Editor
Mara Ellen Guckian

Editorial Project Manager
Ina Massler Levin, M.A.

Editor in Chief
Sharon Coan, M.S. Ed.

Illustrator
Chandler Sinnott

Cover Artist
Jessica Orlando

Art Coordinator
Denice Adorno

Creative Director
Elayne Roberts

Imaging
Ralph Olmedo, Jr.

Product Manager
Phil Garcia

Publishers
Rachelle Cracchiolo, M.S. Ed.
Mary Dupuy Smith, M.S. Ed.

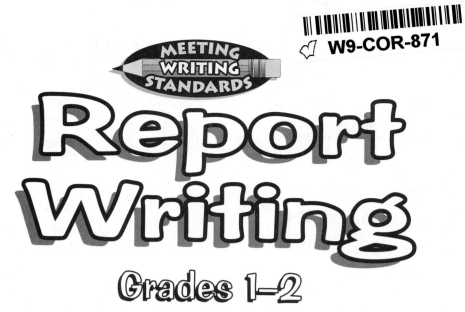

Report Writing

Grades 1–2

Written by

Sarah Kartchner Clark, M.A.

Teacher Created Materials, Inc.
6421 Industry Way
Westminster, CA 92683

www.teachercreated.com

ISBN-1-57690-983-2

©2000 Teacher Created Materials, Inc.
Made in U.S.A.

Table of Contents

Table of Contents *(cont.)*

Introduction

You are about to embark on a unit of study for report writing. This unit is geared for students in first and second grade, or students at similar levels. Report writing at this age is very new. For many students, the animal report written during this unit of study will be their first report. The lessons and activities in this unit are written to give students plenty of practice and opportunities to become familiar with the steps of writing a report and the writing process.

Report Writing has been divided up into sections. Dividing this unit into sections will make it easier to focus on and assess the individual parts of the report writing process. The sections are Brainstorming Your Report, Researching Your Report, Drafting Your Report, Editing Your Report, Publishing Your Report, Mechanics and Grammar, The Inquiry Journal, The Observation Report, and The Oral Report. There are a variety of lessons and activity pages in each section. Appropriate standards and benchmarks are listed at the top of each lesson. You may choose to do all the lessons for each section, or you may select lessons appropriate for the level of your students and your time frame. Use the Teacher Checklist for Report Writing Standards (pages 23–24) to cross reference skills with the lessons being taught. A unit planning sheet (page 10) has been included for your convenience as you plan the lessons and activities in this unit.

It is important for you to make preparations ahead of time for the unit. Look on page 20 for classroom ideas and Daily Doses to incorporate into the unit. Several bulletin board ideas are provided on pages 13–18. These bulletin board examples and ideas will help reinforce the skills being taught in the lessons. Select the bulletin boards you will be using and get materials ready for each of them.

Prior to the unit, create or purchase journals for each student. These can be used as part of the daily doses and as periodic checks on student understanding of the new concepts being taught. To further reinforce concepts, each unit includes home-school activity pages. These are to be sent home to parents and caregivers. These optional activities are designed to reinforce skills being taught at school.

Portfolios (see page 22) are a great way of keeping track of student progress and student work. Assemble portfolios before you begin the unit of study. Keep the portfolios accessible for both the teacher and students alike. Do not store them in the students' desks. They can easily get lost that way. Acknowledge progress and praise student work on a regular basis. Portfolios are essential to document the growth and achievement in the process of writing reports.

Assessment is critical in this unit. Assessment needs to take place at each step of the report writing process. There are three types of assessment in this unit. Each of the first six sections ends with an assessment rubric. The assessment rubrics will help you see how well your students are learning and mastering the standards and objectives. Another form of assessment is sample reports. Sample reports on page 25 provide examples of how students in first and second grade can write reports. Be sure to pull samples from your own class to help establish a standard of competent, emergent, and beginner reports. Finally, the Teacher Checklist for Report Writing Standards on pages 23–24 will be used to record student mastery of standards and benchmarks. The checklist will assist in knowing when to reteach skills and objectives, and will track student progress and achievement.

Standards for Writing
Grades K–2

Accompanying the major activities of this book will be references to the basic standards and benchmarks for writing that will be met by successful performance of the activities. Each specific standard and benchmark will be referred to by the appropriate number and letter from the following collection. For example, a basic standard and benchmark identified as **1A** would be as follows:

Standard 1: Demonstrates competence in the general skills and strategies of the writing process

Benchmark A: Prewriting: Uses prewriting strategies to plan written work (e.g., discusses ideas with peers, draws pictures to generate ideas, writes key thoughts and questions, rehearses ideas, records reactions and observations)

A basic standard and benchmark identified as **4B** would be as follows:

Standard 4: Gathers and uses information for research purposes

Benchmark B: Uses books to gather information for research topics (e.g., uses table of contents, examines pictures and charts)

Clearly, some activities will address more than one standard. Moreover, since there is a rich supply of activities included in this book, some will overlap in the skills they address, and some, of course, will not address every single benchmark within a given standard. Therefore, when you see these standards referenced in the activities, refer to this section for complete descriptions.

Although virtually every state has published its own standards and every subject area maintains its own lists, there is surprising commonality among these various sources. For the purposes of this book, we have elected to use the collection of standards synthesized by John S. Kendall and Robert J. Marzano in their book *Content Knowledge: A Compendium of Standards and Benchmarks for K–12 Education* (Second Edition, 1997) as illustrative of what students at various grade levels should know and be able to do. The book is published jointly by McREL (Mid-continent Regional Educational Laboratory, Inc.) and ASCD (Association for Supervision and Curriculum Development). (Used by permission of McREL.)

Language Arts Standards

1. Demonstrates competence in the general skills and strategies of the writing process

2. Demonstrates competence in the stylistic and rhetorical aspects of writing

3. Uses grammatical and mechanical conventions in written compositions

4. Gathers and uses information for research purposes

Standards for Writing
Grades K–2 *(cont.)*

Level I (Grades K–2)

1. Demonstrates competence in the general skills and strategies of the writing process

A. Prewriting: Uses prewriting strategies to plan written work (e.g., discusses ideas with peers, draws pictures to generate ideas, writes key thoughts and questions, rehearses ideas, records reactions and observations)

B. Drafting and Revising: Uses strategies to draft and revise written work (e.g., rereads; rearranges words, sentences, and paragraphs to improve or clarify meaning; varies sentence types; adds descriptive words and details; deletes extraneous information; incorporates suggestions from peers and teachers; sharpens the focus)

C. Editing and Publishing: Uses strategies to edit and publish written work (e.g., proofreads using a dictionary and other resources; edits for grammar, punctuation, capitalization, and spelling at a developmentally appropriate level; incorporates illustrations or photos; shares finished product)

D. Evaluates own and others' writing (e.g., asks questions and makes comments about writing, helps classmates apply grammatical and mechanical conventions)

E. Dictates or writes with a logical sequence of events (e.g., includes a beginning, middle, and ending)

F. Dictates or writes detailed descriptions of familiar persons, places, objects, or experiences

G. Writes in response to literature

H. Writes in a variety of formats (e.g., picture books, letters, stories, poems, and information pieces)

Standards for Writing
Grades K–2 *(cont.)*

Level I (Grades K–2)

> **2. Demonstrates competence in the stylistic and rhetorical aspects of writing**

   A. Uses general, frequently used words to convey basic ideas

> **3. Uses grammatical and mechanical conventions in written compositions**

   A. Forms letters in print and spaces words and sentences

   B. Uses complete sentences in written compositions

   C. Uses declarative and interrogative sentences in written compositions

   D. Uses nouns in written compositions (e.g., nouns for simple objects, family members, community workers, and categories)

   E. Uses verbs in written compositions (e.g., verbs for a variety of situations, action words)

   F. Uses adjectives in written compositions (e.g., uses descriptive words)

   G. Uses adverbs in written compositions (e.g., uses words that answer how, when, where, and why questions)

   H. Uses conventions of spelling in written compositions (e.g., spells high frequency words and commonly misspelled words from appropriate grade-level list; uses a dictionary and other resources to spell words; spells own first and last name)

   I. Uses conventions of capitalization in written compositions (e.g., first and last names, first word of a sentence)

   J. Uses conventions of punctuation in written compositions (e.g., uses periods after declarative sentences, uses question marks after interrogative sentences, uses commas in a series)

> **4. Gathers and uses information for research purposes**

   A. Generates questions about topics of personal interest

   B. Uses books to gather information for research topics (e.g., uses table of contents, examines pictures and charts)

Frequently Asked Questions

▲ What is report writing?

When you ask your students to write a report, you are asking them to do two things. You are asking them to research and learn information about a topic, and you are asking them to take the information they have learned and share this information in a written report. These are both large tasks but can be done with organization and direction. There are many types of reports, just as there are different types of writing.

▲ Why a unit on how to write reports?

This unit is on report writing for first through second grade. One of the most frustrating writing assignments that a student is given is to write a research report. Teachers struggle getting students to produce well-written reports that use a variety of sources. Part of the reason for this is that the process to write a report is long and cumbersome and uses a multitude of skills. Teachers and students can easily get overwhelmed in the process. This unit will provide a format where the teachers and students can walk through the report writing process while learning and using skills that will help in all areas of writing.

▲ Can primary grade students really write research reports?

Yes, students can with guidance. Students in primary grades are walking information machines. Just ask a first or second grader about dinosaurs, or the latest action figure on television, and most can spill out a plethora of information. Helping them channel and organize their information can be a great tool. Focusing on their interests is the motivation students need to research and learn more about a topic.

▲ What are some common teaching mistakes?

One of the most common mistakes that teachers make is to expect more than a student can do with too little instruction. Many teachers simply give students a date for when their reports are due, along with the requirement for the length of the report. Then they schedule time in the library and wait for the finished product. When the reports come in, they seldom meet the expectations of the teacher. The teacher then in frustration says, "These kids don't know how to write!" Teaching students how to write a report requires teaching them to use the writing process and working with them every step of the way, until they are ready to do the steps independently. Expecting a student to write a report is like expecting a student to ride a bike without any instruction or coaching along the way. Teaching students how to write using the writing process will lead to better writers and students will gain the tools needed to write in other subject areas as well.

▲ Isn't there too much to teach on report writing?

Many times teachers will assign students to write a report with too high of an expectation. Primary grade students need to start small. They should spend more time on learning to research and less time on the report writing as they build their writing skills. Older students, in first and second grade, are ready to write multi-paragraph reports. The suggestion here is to spend more time on less parts of the report writing process. Add more parts of the report writing process and higher expectations as their writing skills and abilities build.

Planning the Report Writing Unit

This report writing unit for Grades 1 and 2 is filled with ways to teach your students how to write a research report. There are varied activities at different skill levels to meet the needs of all students in your class. The topic for this report writing unit is *Animals*. This topic was selected for two reasons. The first reason is that this topic is broad enough to include many of the students' interests. Secondly, this topic has plenty of resources available for students at their own reading and writing level.

You will find this unit divided up into nine sections. Listed below are items found in the sections. You may go through this unit teaching each lesson and activity, or you may select lessons and activities to vary the interest and to meet the needs of your students. You can use the Unit Planner on page 10 to organize and plan your unit. This will help you select lessons and activities, and the timing of each one, to be taught in your classroom.

Lessons

Each section in this unit has lessons to teach and reinforce the objectives being taught. Lessons can be varied and modified.

Learning Centers

Learning Centers provide practice and reinforce the concepts and objectives being taught. Some students need more practice in order to be successful. There are a variety of learning center activities available to provide this practice.

Games

Games are a fun and motivating way to learn. The games in this unit are used to reinforce skills and objectives being taught. Altering some of your own classroom favorites can also do the job.

Home-School Activities

Parents are always wondering how they can better support what is being taught at school. These are optional activities that you can send home for parents to do with their child. Send home the parent letter (page 12) at the beginning of the Report Writing Unit, so that parents will be aware of what the class is studying.

Technology Connections

Technology is especially important in report writing. Therefore, techology connections have been provided when appropriate for the lesson. See page 19 for suggestions on how to incorporate technology into each report writing lesson.

Assessment

Assessment is a critical part of teaching this report writing unit. You will find an assessment rubric at the end of each of the first six sections. These rubrics will allow you to easily assess how well students have mastered a specific part of report writing. You will also find an assessment section with a teacher checklist (pages 23 and 24) containing the complete list of standards. Keeping up to date on these checklists will help you know what standards and benchmarks your students are mastering and what areas need reinforcement and reteaching.

Unit Planner

Date	Standard	Lesson #	Materials Needed

Learning Centers/Materials	Other Resources Needed
Games	

The Writing Process

The *writing process* is the term used to describe the steps a student takes to write a report. Each step of the process is unique and each step is necessary. Listed below are the main objectives and key points of each step in the writing process.

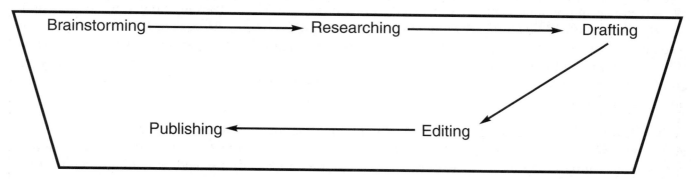

Brainstorming

The brainstorming step is the beginning stage of the report writing process. In this step, a topic is selected and prior knowledge is tapped into in order to provide a beginning. Brainstorming techniques include things such as webbing, clustering, free writing, and more—whatever it takes to get the ideas down on paper. Brainstorming should be done individually as well as in groups, as other students' ideas will trigger new ideas and concepts.

Researching

With an idea in place, students then need to gather new information. There are a variety of resources that students can use to gather this much needed information. Some of these resources include books, encyclopedias, the Internet, dictionaries, newspapers, magazines, people, and more. Once students begin reading and learning more about their topics, they need to jot down notes. Encourage students to take down main ideas and not just copy what is in their resources. Note taking takes practice.

Drafting

At this stage in the writing process, students are ready to focus and organize their ideas and notes. Assist students in deciding what their main focus and idea will be on the animal they are researching. Give clear directions and criteria for students to write their drafts. The criteria established for this unit are a title, a beginning sentence, three middle sentences, and a concluding sentence. You may alter this criteria to meet the needs and the levels of your students.

Editing and Revising

Now comes the polishing part of the report. At this stage, students look back on what they have written and make corrections in spelling, grammar, punctuation, and capitalization. These are the tools needed by effective writers.

Publishing

Publishing occurs when the other steps are completed and the student is ready to write his or her final draft. The final draft can be handwritten, typed, or word processed. The goal is to present the information attractively so others can enjoy it.

Parent Letter

Date _____

Dear Parents,

We are embarking on a new unit of study in the classroom. We will be learning how to write a research report. Our topic will be animals. Students will go through the writing process of brainstorming, researching, writing a draft, editing and revising, and publishing a finished product. There are so many skills that your child will learn in this process. I have included a list of objectives (see below) that your child will be taught in this unit. This unit of study will also include an independent research report, an observation report, and an oral report.

To begin, we will be researching animals. We will be putting together a research center in our classroom. This center will include items such as dictionaries, encyclopedias, thesauruses, nonfiction books about animals, and more. If you have any items at home that you would be willing to let us use in our research center, please let us know.

Periodically throughout this unit, a paper will be sent home with optional activities that you can do at home with your child. You may want to be more involved in the learning process and this is one way that you can. Just asking your child questions about what he or she is researching and learning can be a start. If you have any questions, please don't hesitate to ask.

Sincerely,

_____

Writing Skills Objectives

1. **Demonstrates competence in the general skills and strategies of the writing process**
   A. Prewriting: Uses prewriting strategies to plan written work
   B. Drafting and Revising: Uses strategies to draft and revise written work
   C. Editing and Publishing: Uses strategies to edit and publish written work
   D. Evaluates own and others' writing
   E. Dictates or writes with a logical sequence of events
   F. Dictates or writes detailed descriptions of familiar persons, places, objects, or experiences
   G. Writes in response to literature
   H. Writes in a variety of formats
2. **Demonstrates competence in the stylistic and rhetorical aspects of writing**
   A. Uses general, frequently used words to convey basic ideas
3. **Uses grammatical and mechanical conventions in written compositions**
   A. Forms letters in print and spaces words and sentences
   B. Uses complete sentences in written compositions
   C. Uses declarative and interrogative sentences in written compositions
   D. Uses nouns in written compositions
   E. Uses verbs in written compositions
   F. Uses adjectives in written compositions
   G. Uses adverbs in written compositions
   H. Uses conventions of spelling in written compositions
   I. Uses conventions of capitalization in written compositions
   J. Uses conventions of punctuation in written compositions
4. **Gathers and uses information for research purposes**
   A. Generates questions about topics of personal interest
   B. Uses books to gather information for research topics

Bulletin Board Ideas

Displaying your students' work throughout the unit can be good reinforcement for the skills your students will be learning. Use the bulletin board ideas on the next few pages to highlight the different stages of the report writing process: brainstorming, researching, drafting, editing, and publishing.

Bulletin Board 1

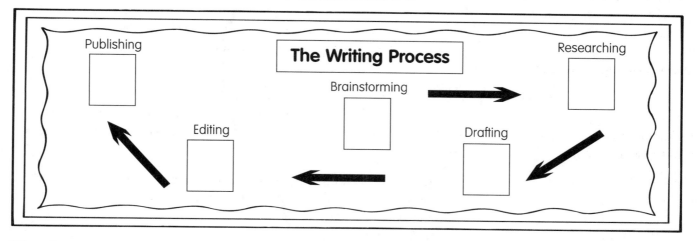

Directions

This bulletin board will show a work in progress! Put colorful paper up as a background and select a colorful border to put up around the edges. In large letters across the top, staple cut-out letters to read, "The Writing Process," and the words, "Brainstorming," "Researching," "Drafting," "Editing," and "Publishing." Staple these letters and arrows to show the writing process. Staple samples of student work for each category as students complete them.

Bulletin Board 2

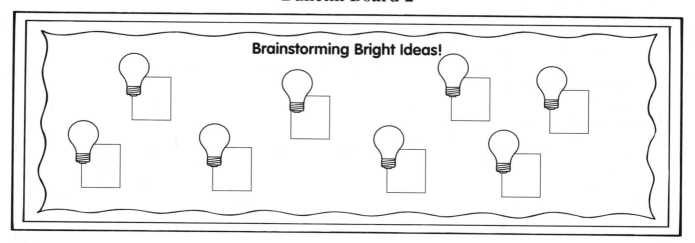

Directions

This bulletin board is an easy way to keep track of ideas for reports. Put colorful paper up as a background and select a colorful border to put up around the edges. Make copies page 14. Have students color the light bulb and write down their brainstorming ideas. Later, have students cut out the bulb and their idea and add them to the bulletin board. In large letters across the top, staple cut-out letters to read, "Brainstorming Bright Ideas!"

Bulletin Board Ideas *(cont.)*

Bright Brainstorming Ideas

_____

_____

_____

_____

_____

_____

Name: _____

Bulletin Board Ideas *(cont.)*

Bulletin Board 3

Directions

Put colorful paper up as a background and select a colorful border to put up around the edges. Make copies of the rocket pattern on page 16 for each student. On the rocket, have students write a sentence or two about the animal they are researching. Cut out the letters and exclamation point for "Researching is a Blast!" and staple them with the rockets to the bulletin board.

Bulletin Board 4

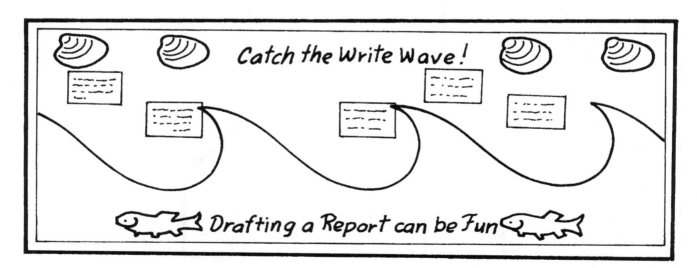

Directions

Put light blue paper up as a background and cut dark blue paper in the shape of waves. Staple the waves on to give it a 3-D look. The border of this bulletin board can be cut-outs of sea shapes such as fish and shells. Post student work in and around the waves. Cut the letters, "Catch the Write Wave!" and "Drafting a Report Can Be Fun!" Then staple them to the bulletin board.

Bulletin Board Ideas *(cont.)*
Rocket

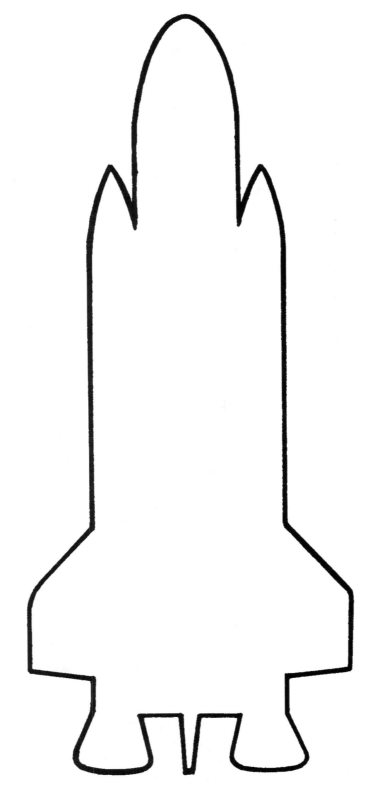

16

Bulletin Board Ideas *(cont.)*

Bulletin Board 5

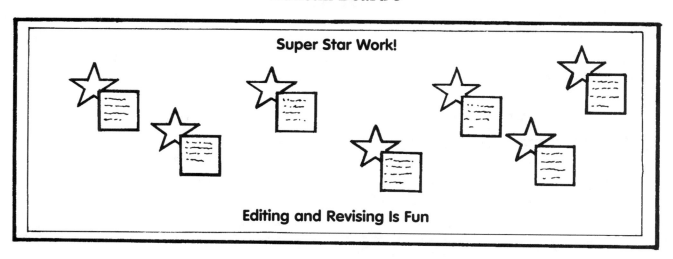

Directions

This bulletin board will reinforce good efforts on the editing work your students are doing. Put blue or black paper up as a background and select a colorful border to put up around the edges. Duplicate the stars on page 18 on yellow paper. Write the names of each student on a star. Staple the star next to a piece of work he or she has done while editing and revising their report. Cut out the letters for "Super Star Work!" and "Editing and Revising Is Fun!" Then staple them with the stars and student work showing their editing and revisions to the bulletin board.

Bulletin Board 6

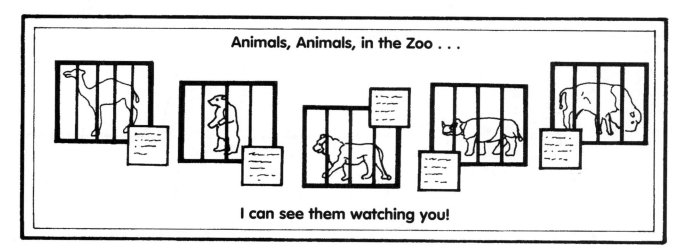

Directions

This bulletin board will spotlight the students' finished reports. Use colorful paper as the background with a colorful border around the edge. Using black paper, make cages to house the animals in the zoo. Have students color a picture of their animal and put them in the "cages." Staple the finished report next to the cage to give information about the animals. Cut out and staple the letters for "Animals, Animals, in the Zoo . . . I can see them watching you!" Staple them to the bulletin board.

Bulletin Board Ideas *(cont.)*

Stars

18

Technology Connections

There are ample opportunities to teach computer and technology skills while teaching the report writing unit. This page lists technology activities that can be used with any lesson. Add them to each lesson in this unit, as needed. You will also need to schedule time to teach your students how to research using the computer. See Teacher Resources on page 142 for information on useful web pages and Internet addresses.

✦ Word Processing

Using a word-processing program, have students type their research topics at the top of the page. Show students how to center these words. Underneath the research topic, have students type words that can be associated with that subject. Students may use their brainstorming webs (see page 28) for a reference. Students may add other words and ideas to their typed lists as needed.

Later, allow students to word process their research notes, rough drafts, and/or final drafts. Show students how to save their information and make changes.

✦ Spell Check

Teach students how to use the spell check function after they have finished typing their reports into the computer. Be sure to discuss with them how the computer may miss certain words that may still be incorrect because they are spelled correctly, but not the right word. For example, "I know I am *write* about this." should read, "I know I am *right* about this."

✦ Printer Savvy

Once students have finished learning to type information into the computer, actually seeing a product of what they produced on the computer can be exciting. Be sure to discuss with students proper ways to use the printer so as not to have paper jams, etc. Set up the procedure for your class. You may choose not to have students try to fix any jams or errors.

✦ Graphic Design

Using *CorelDraw*, *Kid Pix*, or the drawing component of *Microsoft Word* or *AppleWorks*, have students draw pictures of their animals.

✦ Internet Research

With guided help and direction, students will be able to find many resources of interest on the Internet. On the day that you plan to use the Internet, plan to have parents on hand to assist students in using search engines and finding Web sites with information on their animals.

✦ Online Encyclopedias

There are many encyclopedias available as software programs as well as encyclopedias that can be found online.

✦ Online Dictionaries and Thesauruses

Students can look up words online using dictionaries and thesauruses.

✦ Writing Programs

There are many writing programs, such as *Schoolhouse Rock!*, that can help reinforce writing skills, as well as provide easy-to-use formats for computer processing.

Daily Doses

This section of the unit provides opportunities for the students to share what they are learning in the report writing process. Daily Doses are sprinkled throughout the day and are not part of a lesson or instruction given on report writing. This will keep them from seeming mundane or routine. Use the Daily Doses suggestions below or create some of your own.

Fact-a-Day

Place a dictionary, a thesaurus, or an encyclopedia on a student's desk each morning before students come into class. The student with the book on his or her desk gets to share a fact that he or she learned about his or her research topic. Students will be excited to see who the lucky person is each morning.

Thumbs Up! You're Up!

This famous game is always fun. Use it as a motivator while students are researching topics. Play the game by having students put their heads down and their thumbs up. A predetermined number of students are selected to be "It." Each of those who are "It" touches the thumb of one of the students with their heads down. When all who are "It" have touched somebody, tell the class to put their heads up. Before they guess who touched them, they have to name two or more facts they have learned about their research topic. If they guess who touched their thumb, the person who is "It" sits down and the new player joins the "It" group. Play continues this way until all students have had a turn.

Question at the Door

Every morning before your students walk into the classroom, post a question on the door of your classroom. The question might be related to the topic one of your students is studying or it might be a general research question. This activity will get students thinking the minute they walk through the door. Look at the examples below:

- Do you know how tall a baby giraffe is when born?
- Do you know where the Great Barrier Reef is located?

Daily Research Sentences

Give each student two or three slips of paper. Have each student write a different fact he or she has learned about his or her research topic. Have them write each one on a different slip of paper. Place all the slips of paper in a jar. Each day, draw out two slips of paper and write both facts on the board. As you write them, intentionally misspell words and leave out punctuation and capitalization, or make other errors. Students are to write the sentences and correct all errors. This will encourage researching as well as teach editing skills.

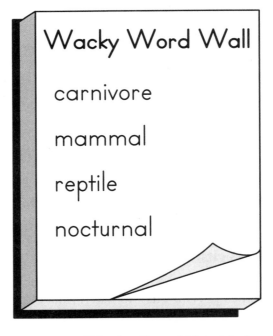

Wacky Word Wall

Designate an area of your classroom wall as the Wacky Word Wall. Post a large piece of paper. Any time a student finds a new word while researching, have him or her write the word on the paper. Students will increase their vocabulary along with researching skills.

Journal Writing

Allowing students to talk and write about what they are learning will help cement concepts and objectives. At the beginning of the unit, purchase or make journals for students to use. At a specified time of the day, have students respond to a journal topic. Listed below are some suggestions. You and your students may also have other topics to add to the list. Feel free to modify topics, as needed.

1. The thing I like about my research topic/animal is . . .

2. The question I am most interested in right now is . . .

3. The new thing I have learned while doing this report writing is . . .

4. The thing I wish I could change about my research topic is . . .

5. The hardest thing for me to do in researching is . . .

6. I think a good writer . . .

7. The things I like to write about are . . .

8. Some of the things that make me a good writer are . . .

9. Some of the things I need to work on in my writing are . . .

10. The things I don't like writing about are . . .

11. The best thing I ever wrote was . . .

12. The type of writing I like to do is . . .

13. The type of writing I like to read is . . .

14. Something I learned about myself and my writing is . . .

15. I wish I could write a letter to . . .

16. Kids need to write more because . . .

17. I think my writing is important when . . .

18. The thing I learned the most about when doing the research report was . . .

19. The questions I still have about my research topic animal are . . .

Portfolio Assessment

Because writing a report is a process, using a portfolio is the best way to show student progress. Portfolios also allow students a means to demonstrate their understanding of each step in the report writing process. A portfolio can be made with a three-ring folder or binder. There should be a portfolio for each student. Write the name of the student on the outside of the folder so it can be easily located. Keep the portfolios in a basket or box on a counter so you and your students can access them easily. Keep samples of student work throughout this report writing unit. Be sure to include samples of each stage in the writing process including brainstorming, researching, rough draft, editing, revising, and publishing.

Keep the Following Points in Mind When Using Portfolios:

- The portfolio belongs to the student. Encourage students to take pride in their work. Be careful of the notes and comments that you make on student work. Be sure that the comments are dignified and encouraging. Nobody wants to save and repeatedly look at an assignment with negative comments on it.

- Add samples regularly, but not too often. It is important to get a thorough sample of each step in the report writing process, but too many papers and samples can be overwhelming to organize.

- Add a variety of samples documenting each phase of the writing process. Selecting the best example of each stage in the process may give a better picture of what the student is able to do, but including beginning samples of a stage as well as more developed samples can show progress.

- Review portfolios frequently. Be sure to include times to look through the portfolios. Giving students suggestions on what to look for as they review their portfolios is an effective way to use the portfolio. Don't just ask students to look through their portfolios. Point out progress and insights to their writing process. Be their guide as they learn about themselves as writers.

- Note the progress of each student. Be sure to set up times to meet individually with each student. Acknowledge and praise progress. Discuss suggestions for each student to improve his or her writing. Be concise. Don't give too many suggestions, as your message may get lost.

- Share with parents. Allow parents to review the portfolio. You may have a homework assignment for students to review their portfolios with parents. Encourage parents to write positive comments about their child's writing and progress.

- Allow time for students to write or dictate a reflection about their writing and their writing abilities. These reflections will show progression and growth as well.

Teacher Checklist for Report Writing Standards

Name: _____

Skill	First Attempt	Mastery
1. Demonstrates competence in the general skills and strategies of the writing process		
Prewriting		
A. Uses Prewriting Strategies to plan written work		
discusses ideas with peers		
draws pictures to generate ideas		
writes key thoughts and questions		
rehearses ideas		
records reactions and observations		
Drafting and Revising		
B. Uses strategies to draft and revise written work		
rereads		
rearranges words, sentences, and paragraphs to improve or clarify meaning		
varies sentence types		
adds descriptive words and details		
deletes extraneous information		
incorporates suggestions from peers and teachers		
sharpens the focus		
Editing and Publishing		
C. Uses strategies to edit and publish written work		
proofreads using a dictionary and other resources		
edits for grammar, punctuation, capitalization, and spelling at appropriate developmental level		
incorporates illustrations or photos		
shares finished product		
D. Evaluates own and others' writing		
asks questions and makes comments about writing		
helps classmates apply grammatical and mechanical conventions		
E. Dictates or writes with a logical sequence of events (i.e., includes a beginning, middle, & end)		
F. Dictates or writes detailed descriptions of familiar persons, places, objects, or experiences		
G. Writes in response to literature		
H. Writes in a variety of formats (e. g., picture books, letters, stories, poems, information pieces)		

Teacher Checklist for Report Writing Standards (cont.)

Name: _____

Skill	First Attempt	Mastery
2. Demonstrates competence in the stylistic and rhetorical aspects of writing		
A. Uses general, frequently used words to convey basic ideas		
3. Uses grammatical and mechanical conventions in written composition		
A. Forms letters in print and spaces words and sentences		
B. Uses complete sentences in written compositions		
C. Uses declarative and interrogative sentences in written compositions		
D. Uses nouns in written compositions		
E. Uses verbs in written compositions		
F. Uses adjectives in written compositions		
G. Uses adverbs in written compositions		
H. Uses conventions of spelling in written compositions		
spells high frequency words, commonly misspelled words		
uses a dictionary and other resources to spell words		
spells own first and last name		
I. Uses conventions of capitalization in written compositions		
first and last names		
first word in each sentence		
J. Uses conventions of punctuation in written compositions		
uses periods after declarative sentences		
uses question marks after interrogative sentences		
uses commas in a series		
4. Gathers and uses information for research purposes		
A. Generates questions about topics of personal interest		
B. Uses books to gather information for research topics		
uses table of contents		
examines pictures and charts		

Sample Reports for Grades 1 and 2

These reports are to be used as samples only. Students in your class may be above or below the levels of these sample reports. Pull samples from your own class to help you establish a standard of competent, emergent, and beginner reports.

Competent

The report has a centered and underlined title. The report begins with an interrogative sentence to interest the reader. There are detailed sentences with correct information on a variety of subjects showing that research has been done. The report has correct punctuation, capitalization, and spelling. The report closes with an ending sentence. The report is neat and easy to read.

> ## The Crayfish
>
> Did you know a crayfish looks like a lobster? Crayfish live in lakes and rivers. Lobsters live in the ocean. Crayfish can only live in clean water. A crayfish has a protective outer coat. This helps keep the crayfish safe. Crayfish can grow new legs if one comes off. Crayfish are so interesting!

Emergent

This report has a lot of good sentences, but needs work on using capital letters and spelling certain words correctly. The report has a title, but it needs to be centered. This report could use a more developed beginning, middle, and ending.

> the crayfish
>
> a crayfish has a outer coat crayfish looks like the lobster. crayfish are interesting. crayfish live i n lakes and rivers. crayfish loive in Clean water. it helps keep the crayfish safe. cray fish can gorow new legs if one comes of.

Beginner

This report needs help with a title, capitalization, punctuation, spelling, and complete sentences. The report contains inventive spelling. There is no logical sequence in this report. The student may need to dictate a report and rewrite what is written.

> cfrayfish eat crayfish lif in laks an rivers crafish live in celan wter gro legs it sohdne. legios grow from saff

Brainstorming Your Report

Brainstorming is the first step in the report writing process. Brainstorming is collecting ideas by thinking openly and freely about all possibilities. Brainstorming is most often used in groups, but can be done very effectively by an individual student who is gathering thoughts and ideas to write a report.

This section of the unit has lessons for different types of brainstorming techniques. Some of the techniques include webbing, using the KWL format, discussing ideas with peers, and using drawings and illustrations.

All or some of these lessons may be used to have students begin the report writing process.

Standards and Benchmarks: 1A

Brainstorming Lesson 1

Objective

The student will use the brainstorming technique of discussing ideas with peers as a prewriting strategy.

Materials

- copy of the Brainstorming Web (page 28) for each student
- large piece of paper taped to the chalkboard at the front of the classroom with pictures of animals from magazines or other sources taped around its edges
- tape

Procedure

1. Discuss with students what the word *brainstorming* means. Explain that there are no wrong answers when brainstorming.

2. Tell students that you will be writing for them so that their brains can concentrate on thinking. Write the word *animal* in the center of the large piece of paper. Encourage students to say whatever comes to mind when they think of the word *animal*. Record all their answers in a web format. Have students raise their hands so that you can keep track of all the responses.

3. Do this as long as ideas are coming from the students. Then, begin asking questions about their responses. Here are some possible questions: *What made you think of . . . ? Are there things that are similar? Are there things that are different? Are there some things on our chart that you didn't think of before? What do you like about brainstorming?*

4. Now distribute a copy of the brainstorming web to each student. Have them pick an animal in which they are interested. Have students write the name of the animal in the center of the brainstorming web. Then have students write words or ideas they can think of about this animal. Some spelling errors may occur, but the point is to get the words and ideas down.

5. When students have completed their graphic, divide them into groups of two. The first student shares his or her animal and the words he or she came up with to go with the animal. The second student listens and suggests other ideas that could also be associated with that animal. The first student may add the new ideas or words if he or she likes. Now, the students switch roles and the second student shares his or her work.

Portfolio Piece

Have students write their names and the date at the top of their webs and then place them in their portfolios. This is the beginning of the research report writing process.

Assessment

- Check to see that students have completed the brainstorming web.
- Check off the appropriate prewriting strategy skill (1A) on the Teacher Checklist on page 23 of the Assessment Section. Assess student work using the Brainstorming Assessment Rubric on page 38.

Brainstorming Web

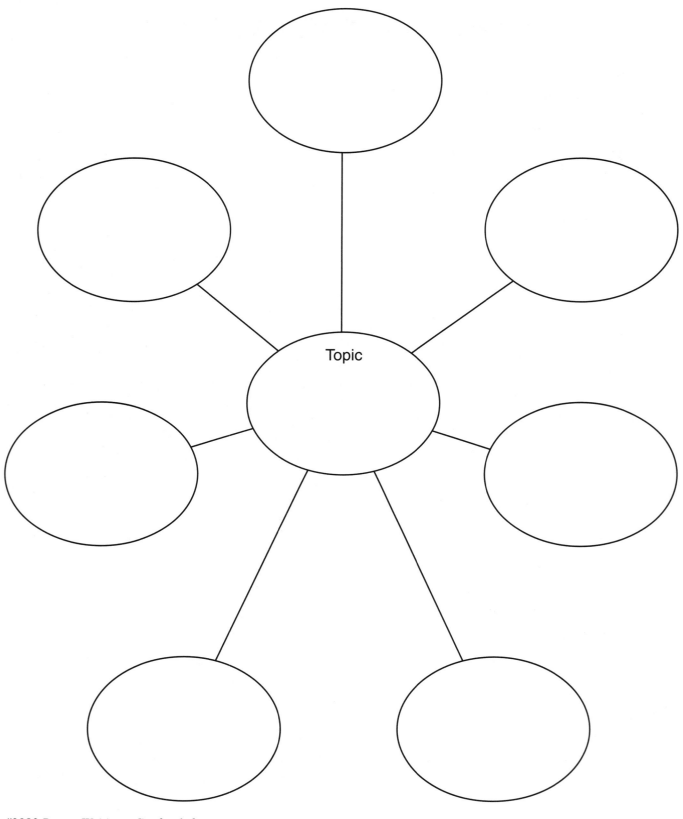

Topic

Standards and Benchmarks: 1A

Brainstorming Lesson 2

Objective

The student will use the brainstorming technique of drawing pictures to generate ideas as a prewriting strategy.

Materials

- piece of white paper for each student
- crayons or colored pencils for each student
- cassette tape or CD of jungle or nature music (optional)

Procedure

1. Explain to students that they will be using pictures to help them learn more about the animals that they have chosen.

2. Have students draw a picture of the animal that they will be researching and studying. Then have them draw smaller pictures about the animal around the edges. The small pictures might be what the animal eats, where it lives, or any other information that the student already knows about the animal. Instruct students that these are real pictures, not pretend pictures. Play the cassette or CD of nature music as background music to help the students visualize their animals.

3. After students have finished drawing their pictures, divide the class into groups of three or four students. Have students take turns sharing their pictures and discussing what they drew with the other group members. Allow students to ask questions and give positive feedback.

4. Lead a discussion about the pictures they have drawn about their animal. Ask some questions like the following:

   - By looking at your pictures, what do you already know about your animal?
   - Did you know what color to draw your animal?
   - Did you know where the animal lives?
   - Did you know what the animal eats?
   - Is your animal tame or wild?

Portfolio Piece

Have students write their names and the date at the top, and then place their drawings in their portfolios.

Assessment

- Check to see that each student has completed the drawing of his or her animal.
- Check off the appropriate prewriting strategy skill (1A) on the Teacher Checklist on page 23 of the Assessment Section. Assess student work using the Brainstorming Assessment Rubric on page 38.

Standards and Benchmarks: 1A

Brainstorming Lesson 3

Objective

The student will use the brainstorming technique of writing key thoughts and questions as a prewriting strategy.

Materials

- copy of KWL page for each student (page 31)
- sample copy of a research report for each student (Use a sample from a previous student or one you have written.)

Procedure

1. Explain to students that they will be writing a research paper on the animal that they selected in Lesson 2. Show students the sample research report. Explain that they will become experts on the animal they are studying.

2. Use the brainstorming webs students have in their portfolios with their initial key thoughts and ideas about the animal of their choice. Explain that to write a research report, students will be sharing information they already know about their animal and learning new information as well.

3. Make the following chart on the chalkboard:

Know	Want to Know	Learned

In the **Know** column, students will be writing down things they already know about their animals. In the **Want to Know** column, students will ask questions about their animals. In the **Learned** column, students will write down things that they learned after studying their animals.

Do a sample of a KWL chart together as a class. Write *Dogs* in the blank at the top. Under the Know column, record things that students already know about dogs. Under the Want to Know column, record questions or things students want to know about dogs. Explain that you will be saving the Learned column for later.

4. Now have students fill in the blank at the top of their KWL page, and have them fill out their KWL chart, as instructed, on their own animal. Students may use the brainstorming webs in their portfolios for reference, if needed.

Portfolio Piece

Have students write the date at the top, and then place their KWL pages in their portfolios. They will need to fill out the last column at the end of writing their research report.

Assessment

- Check to see that students have completed the KWL page correctly.
- Check off the appropriate prewriting strategy skill (1A) on the Teacher Checklist on page 23 of the Assessment Section. Assess student work using the Brainstorming Assessment Rubric on page 38.

KWL

Topic: _____

K (Know)	W (Want to Know)	L (Learned)

Standards and Benchmarks: 1A, 4A

Brainstorming Lesson 4

Objective

The student will use the brainstorming technique of writing key thoughts and questions as a prewriting strategy.

Materials

- copy of the Research Cube for each student, page 33
- crayons or colored pencils for each student
- scissors for each student
- glue
- magazines with pictures of animals
- yarn or string to hang the research cubes

Procedure

1. This activity helps the students record the questions they have about their research topics. Have students cut out the research cubes. Next, have students write down questions they have about their animals in each square. Each side of the cube should have a different question each student wants to learn about his or her animal.

2. Students can then illustrate their questions with crayons, colored pencils, or cutout pictures from magazines that would go with their animal.

3. Cut out the cubes, glue the edges together, and hang the cubes from the ceiling when they are completed. Students may refer to their cubes to see what things they wanted to learn about their research topics.

Portfolio Piece

Have students write or dictate a reflection in their portfolio about how they feel about learning information about the animal they chose. What are some thoughts and questions they have about this animal? Date and place the reflections in the students' portfolios.

Assessment

- Check to see that students have completed the research cube completely and neatly.
- Check off the appropriate prewriting strategy skills (1A, 4A) on the Teacher Checklist on pages 23 and 24 of the Assessment Section.
- Assess student work using the Brainstorming Assessment Rubric on page 38.

Research Cube

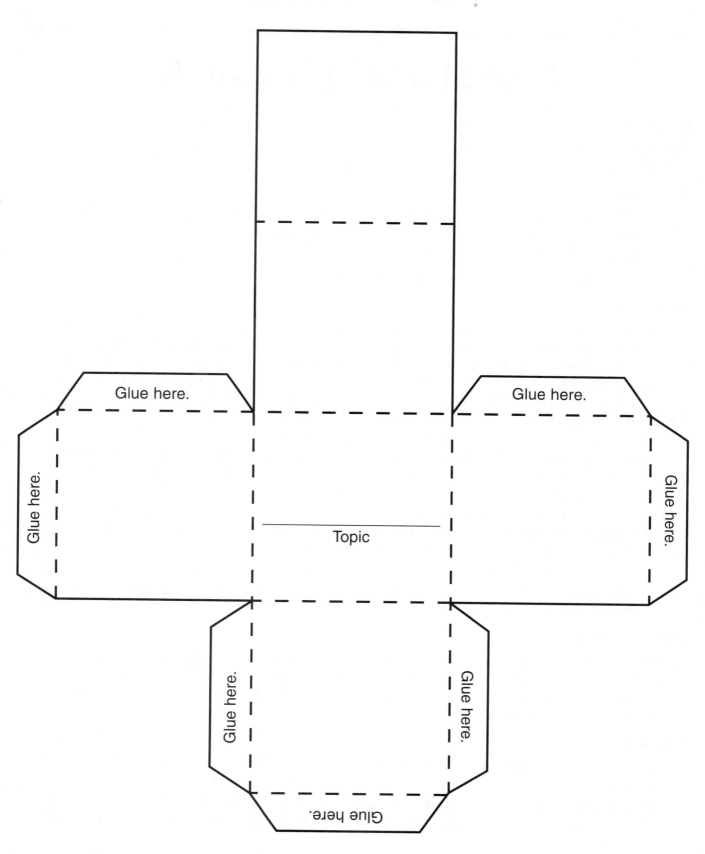

Glue here.

Glue here.

Glue here.

Glue here.

Topic

Glue here.

Glue here.

Glue here.

Standards and Benchmarks: 1A

Brainstorming Lesson 5

Objective

The student will use the brainstorming technique of recording reactions and observations as a prewriting strategy.

Materials

- resource materials on animals, including books, posters, magazines, encyclopedias, stuffed animals, computer graphics, newspaper articles, or any other items
- animal sounds tape or CD (optional)
- paper or small notebook (optional) for each student

Procedure

1. Ahead of time, set aside a room or use your own room to create an Experience Room. This room is dedicated to the study of animals. Set up displays all over the room of books, magazines, posters, stuffed animals, postcards, newspaper articles, and any other animal resources. Hang posters and pictures of animals, play background music, and do anything you can think of to create an atmosphere of learning about animals. Decorate the room to invite students to want to learn. Arrange reading areas where students can sit and look at items.

2. Before taking students to the Experience Room, explain to them that they are going to be researchers. Explain that researchers look for information, ask questions, and learn as they go. Instruct students to keep an open mind about what they will see and hear. Instruct students to treat resources and displays with respect.

3. Give each student a piece of paper or a notebook. They are to write questions, observations, thoughts, ideas, and reactions to the information surrounding them. They will be using these notes to help them select an animal for a research topic.

4. Enter the Experience Room with students and allow time for them to observe, record, read, learn, and digest the information in the room about animals. Be sure to allow students time to get to all of the resource materials available.

Portfolio Piece

Have students write or dictate a reflection in their portfolios about how they felt in the Experience Room. What did they like about it? What did they learn? What animal do they think they want to study? What are some thoughts and questions they have about this animal? Date and place the reflections in the students' portfolios.

Assessment

- Check to see that students are recording information and observations in their notebooks or on their paper.
- Check off the appropriate prewriting strategy skill (1A) on the Teacher Checklist on page 23 of the Assessment Section. Assess student work using the Brainstorming Assessment Rubric on page 38.

Standards and Benchmarks: 1A

Brainstorming Learning Centers

Brainstorming Bash

Write the names of different animals on each of about 20 index cards. Place the cards in a pile face down. Using mini whiteboards or chalkboards, have students draw a card from the pile and brainstorm as many words associated with the animal that they can think of in one minute. (The time may vary according to the level of your students.) You can use this activity as a simple brainstorming practice, or you can make it competitive by making the student with the most words the winner after each round.

ABC Research

Give each student a page with the first letter of the animal he or she is researching printed at the top of the page. Students are to write the name of their animal and draw a picture of the animal. Around the animals, they can write other words they think of when they hear their animal's name. Allow students who finish early to take letter pages that are not being used and look up an animal that begins with the needed letter. At the end of the week, after all students have finished their ABC pages at this center, staple them together and create a book. Write "Animal Discoveries" or a title of your own choosing on the title page. Place this book in your class library for students to review. As students read the book, they can add facts and details on the back side of their pages as they learn about their animals.

Brainstorming Word Bank

This simple activity will help build vocabulary as well as provide brainstorming practice. On a large piece of paper, draw or cut a picture of an animal out of a magazine and place it in the center. Make at least four to five of these with different pictures in the middle. Place the charts on a table with markers or crayons. As students come to this learning center, have them write down words they think of when they see these pictures. Post these charts around the classroom for students to use.

"Sticking Up" for Brainstorming

This is a quiet and thought-provoking brainstorming activity. On small pieces of paper, write the names of different animals and place them in a cup. Leave a supply of yellow sticky notes and pencils at this learning center. As students come to this center, one student draws a slip of paper with an animal on it. This is shared with the small group. Have the students place the animal sticky note down in the center of the table. Each person then writes a different idea on a sticky note that is associated with this animal. Without talking, students write their idea on the sticky note and place them around the slip of paper in the center of the table. There is no talking until all students have written and posted their ideas. Students can then talk about their ideas and the connections they made with other students.

Webbing Practice

Make copies of the Brainstorming Web on page 28 and place them at a center along with markers and crayons. Have students write different animals or topics at the center of the web and write ideas and concepts related to that topic.

Standards and Benchmarks: 1A, 4A

Home-School Activities

Here are some *optional* brainstorming activities that you can do at home. These activities will enrich objectives and lessons being taught in school. If you have any questions, please don't hesitate to ask.

✓ Talking and Listening

Invite your child to talk to you about his or her research topic. Be sure to listen to what your child is saying. When finished, ask your child a few questions about the topic to let him or her know you are interested in his or her learning. Be sure to ask your child periodically throughout the research project about what he or she has learned.

✓ Brainstorming-a-Guess

For this activity, you are going to need a piece of paper and a pencil. Select an item from a room in your house. Write down five things about that item. Then go to another room. Select another item. Write down five things about the new item. Go to at least four rooms, select an item, and then write down five things. Meet back together and share your brainstorms. Do this by having your child choose a room. Have your child say the five things he or she brainstormed about the item. See if you can guess the item. Do this with each room/object and then switch. See if your child can guess your items using the brainstorming clues you came up with.

✓ Family Fact Finding Fun

Find ideas for report topics by looking around your neighborhood, your park, your school, and your town. Choose one topic to brainstorm about as a family a few minutes before bed. See if you can come up with at least ten things brainstormed about your topic.

✓ Researching the News

Look for ideas to research when reading the newspaper, reading magazines, or watching television. Keep a folder of notes, clippings, and other information on topics in which your family has an interest. Have your child be in charge of the folder. Discuss the news items or other topics over the dinner table or on car trips.

✓ Brainstorming Charades

Write topics of interest on slips of paper. Family members draw a slip of paper and act out what is written on the paper using the information they already know about the topic. Once the topic has been guessed, discuss the topic as a family. What do other family members know about the subject?

Standards and Benchmarks: 1A

Brainstorming Games

Go for Five

Divide students into teams of four or five students. Write animals or topics on index cards. Place the cards face down in a pile. Draw the first card and read the animal or topic. The teams then work together to brainstorm at least five things associated with the animal or topic. The first team to come up with five wins a point. Continue playing this way until all the cards are used up.

Pass the Word

Divide students into two teams. Write animals or topics on index cards. Have two students from each team come up to the front of the room. One of the students in each pair will be the *brainstormer*, while the other student in the pair will be the *guesser*. Show the brainstormer the card and have him or her give clues that are associated with that animal. The guesser uses the clues to guess what the animal is. The first pair of students to guess the animal correctly wins a point. The game is continued until all students on both teams have had a turn to be a brainstormer and a guesser.

Balloon Bonanza

Blow up a balloon for each student. Write the name of a different animal on each balloon. Do the following activities with the balloons:

- Have students toss their balloons up in the air. The object is to keep the balloons from falling to the ground. Each time a student hits the balloon back up into the air, the student must say something he or she can brainstorm about the animal written on the balloon. After a few minutes, rotate the balloons.

- Place students in pairs facing each other. At your signal, have students play catch with the balloon. When students catch the balloon, they have to say one thing about the animal.

- Have a relay with the balloons. Have students form two lines. Give the first person in each line a balloon. When you say, "Go," the first student says a word or idea associated with the animal written on the balloon and passes it over his or her head to the person behind him or her. The balloon cannot be passed until the idea or word has been said. The first team to pass the balloon this way to the end of the line is the winner. Switch balloons and try this again with different animals.

Chalkboard Relay

Divide your class into groups of two or more, as needed. Line students up in the classroom. Divide the chalkboard up into the amount of groups you have. Write a topic across the top. This may be an animal or something else you are studying in class. Have each team send one student up to the chalkboard. At your signal, each team member is to brainstorm something to write about the topic written across the top of the chalkboard. The student writes his or her brainstorm or thought and places the chalk back down on the chalkboard tray. As soon as the chalk is on the tray, the next member of the team can come up and write his or her brainstorm. A new idea has to be written by each team member. Play continues until every team member has come up to write an idea.

Brainstorming Assessment Rubric

Use the rubric below to assess student progress using the brainstorming techniques. The numbers and letters in parenthesis correspond with the Teacher Checklist (pages 23 and 24) in the Assessment Section.

Competent

The student can independently use prewriting strategies to plan written work. (1A)

The student can independently discuss ideas with peers.

The student can independently draw pictures to generate ideas.

The student can independently write key thoughts and questions.

The student can independently rehearse ideas.

The student can independently record reactions and observations.

The student can independently generate questions about topics of personal interest. (4A)

Emergent

The student can usually use prewriting strategies to plan written work. (1A)

The student can usually discuss ideas with peers.

The student can usually draw pictures to generate ideas.

The student can usually write key thoughts and questions.

The student can usually rehearse ideas.

The student can usually record reactions and observations.

The student can usually generate questions about topics of personal interest. (4A)

Beginner

The student requires assistance to use prewriting strategies to plan written work. (1A)

The student requires assistance to discuss ideas with peers.

The student requires assistance to draw pictures to generate ideas.

The student requires assistance to write key thoughts and questions.

The student requires assistance to rehearse ideas.

The student requires assistance to record reactions and observations.

The student requires assistance to generate questions about topics of personal interest. (4A)

Researching Your Report

Researching the report can be the most fascinating part of the report writing process for students. Allow plenty of time for students to browse and look at the research materials they are using. Remember to allow students time to share with a partner some of the discoveries they are making as they research their animals. Verbalizing these ideas and thoughts will help students begin to know what they want to write about the animals they are studying.

This section of the unit has lessons for using many resources for research. One of the resources is the Internet. If you have access to the Internet, you will find valuable resources there. Be sure to have parents help with this endeavor.

Standards and Benchmarks: 4B

Researching Lesson 1

Objective

The student will use resources found in a library to gather information on a research topic.

Materials

- access to a library with encyclopedias, nonfiction books, and other research materials
- copy of the Library Tour on page 41 for each student

Procedure

1. This activity will teach students how to research using the materials and books available in most libraries. Make arrangements ahead of time to have your school librarian take your class on a tour of the library. (If you do not have a librarian, be sure to familiarize yourself with what is available so that you can take your students on the tour.) Discuss the level and abilities of your students with the librarian so that he or she can teach to their level. Be sure to also let your librarian know what research topics your students have so that he or she can gear the tour towards materials that would be helpful for their topics. Your librarian will also want to go over the proper procedures and behavior needed in order to use materials in the library.

2. Make the trip to the library. Keep the tour short so that students have time to be exposed but not bored with things that are available for them to use in their research. After the tour, allow time for students to explore the resources.

3. After students have had some time to browse, distribute the Library Tour work sheet for students to complete in the library using the research materials.

4. Return to the classroom and discuss the answers to the work sheet. Have a class discussion about their experience at the library. Ask students if they know where they need to look in the library for information on their research topics. Have them turn to a partner and take turns explaining what the process would be to gather information on their research topics in the library. Allow both students a chance to share their plans.

5. Schedule another time in the library for students to conduct research.

Portfolio Piece

Have students write or dictate a reflection in their portfolio about what they learned in the library. What are some books that they think would be really interesting to use in their research projects? Date and place the reflections in the students' portfolios.

Assessment

- Check to see that students have completed the Library Tour page correctly.
- Check off the appropriate research strategy skill (4B) on the Teacher Checklist on page 24 of the Assessment Section. Assess student work using the Research Assessment Rubric on page 52.

Library Tour

1. What book can you use to find the meaning of a word? _____

   _____

   _____

2. What is an encyclopedia?_____

   _____

   _____

3. What is a nonfiction book? _____

   _____

   _____

4. Where are the books about animals located in our school library?

   _____

   _____

5. Where is the reference section in our school library? _____

   _____

   _____

6. Who is our school librarian? _____

   _____

Standards and Benchmarks: 4B

Researching Lesson 2

Objective

The student will use pictures and charts to take notes to gather research information.

Materials

- age-appropriate book with information about animals
- copy of Note-taking Practice for each student (page 43)

Procedure

1. Explain to students that you will be teaching them to take notes, so that they can gather information about the animal they are researching. Note taking takes practice, and students need to be taught how to do it. Begin by discussing the materials needed to take notes. The materials needed are a book or other resource about the topic, a piece of paper, and a sharpened pencil. Distribute the Note-taking Practice sheet to each student, and be sure each student has a sharpened pencil.

2. To take notes, one needs to record information that he or she is learning from a book. Some notes can be done with words, and some note taking is done by drawing sketches and pictures. Explain that while you share a book about animals with the class, students will be taking notes by writing words or drawing pictures about what they see and hear.

3. Show students the front cover of the book. Discuss the picture on the front if there is one. What does the title teach us about the book? What does the picture teach us? Explain that they will be learning from the book and recording the new information on the note-taking page.

4. Read the first page of the book. Allow students plenty of time to look at the pictures and to write down their notes and sketches. Do this for each page, allowing plenty of time for students to record information, but not so much time that many in the class get bored.

5. At the end of the book, have students share their note-taking pages with each other. Have them work in pairs to discuss similarities and differences. After each student has had a chance to share his or her information, discuss the notes as a class. Some of the questions you might ask could include the following: *Why are the notes different? When is it good to draw a picture of what you're learning? When is it good to use words? What did you learn from the book? Do your notes help you remember what you learned?*

Portfolio Piece

Date and place students notes in their portfolios. This is a critical piece of the report writing process.

Assessment

- Check to see that students have taken notes on their note-taking pages.
- Check off the appropriate research strategy skill (4B) on the Teacher Checklist on page 24 of the Assessment Section. Assess student work using the Research Assessment Rubric on page 52.

Note-taking Practice

Name: _____ **Date:** _____

Draw a picture of each of the materials you need to take notes.

Title of the book: _____

Author of the book: _____

Draw or write what you learned from the book.

Standards and Benchmarks: 4B

Researching Lesson 3

Objective

The student will use books to gather information on a research topic.

Materials

- access to a library with encyclopedias, nonfiction books, and other resource materials
- piece of paper and a pencil for each student

Procedure

1. Schedule a time, if needed, for your students to use the library for researching purposes. Remind students of proper library behavior and procedures before you go. Remind students of the note-taking skills learned in Lesson 2.

2. Distribute a piece of paper to each student. Have them fold the paper into fourths. These will be the note-taking pages for students to use in the library. They are to find four things to take notes about. They may use words and pictures.

3. Assist students in locating books, encyclopedias, and other materials to research their animals. Tell students to read what they can but to also use the pictures to teach them about their animals. Circulate around the library to assist each student in his or her reading or writing needs. Remember to allow students time to look and discover information.

4. Return to the classroom and discuss their findings as a class. Each student will want a turn to share his or her latest information. Divide students into groups of four or five. Designate a chair to be the hot seat. Students take turns sitting in the hot seat and sharing with the students the information they gathered. They may use their note-taking sheets, as needed. Allow students to ask each other questions after the report has been given. Giving students a chance to share and discuss the information will help clarify for them what they have learned. Have a class discussion about their experience at the library.

5. Schedule more time in the library for students to research, as needed. Be sure to allow plenty of time in your lesson plans for this.

Portfolio Piece

Date and place students' notes in their portfolios. This is a critical piece of the research report process. Keep all notes in the portfolio for future use.

Technology Connection

Using a word-processing program, have students type in the notes they gathered about their animals while researching in the library.

Assessment

- Check to see that students have taken notes on their note-taking page.
- Check off the appropriate research strategy skill (4B) on the Teacher Checklist on page 24 of the Assessment Section. Assess student work using the Research Assessment Rubric on page 52.

Standards and Benchmarks: 4B

Researching Lesson 4

Objective

The student will use a table of contents to find information in a book.

Materials

- an age-appropriate book that has a table of contents for each student
- access to a library with reference books and other books used for research
- copy of the Table of Contents work sheet (page 46) for each student

Procedure

1. Distribute copies of the page, Table of Contents. Explain that books have a page that helps us find what we are looking for in a book. Write *Table of Contents* across the chalkboard. Have a book available for each student to look at at this time.

2. Have students look inside their books to find the table of contents. Have them keep their fingers in their books to mark the place until all students find the table of contents. Explain that a table of contents lists all the subjects in the book and the pages on which they can be found. Most books that share information have a table of contents.

3. Ask students to locate topics in their books. What are some of these topics? On what pages can these topics be found? Have students practice choosing a topic, seeing the page on which it is found, and locating the page in the book. It can be very difficult for some students to find the pages. Be available for assistance and be sure that the books your students are using are not too long or too difficult.

4. Go over the four questions found on the Table of Contents page. Check to be sure that students understand the questions and allow students time to complete the work sheet. Circulate around the room to offer assistance, as needed.

5. Schedule a time, if necessary, for your students to use the library for researching purposes. Remind students of proper library behavior and procedures before you go.

6. Assist students in locating books, encyclopedias, and other materials to research their animals. Have students look for books that have information about their animals. Next, have students look in the table of contents of each book to determine whether there is information in the book on their research animals. Allow students time to practice using the table of contents. Students may check out books they find that have information about their research animal. Schedule more time in the library for students to research, as needed.

Assessment

- Check to see that students have completed the Table of Contents page correctly.

- Check off the appropriate research strategy skill (4B) on the Teacher Checklist on page 24 of the Assessment Section. Assess student work using the Research Assessment Rubric on page 52.

Table of Contents

1. What is a table of contents?

   _____

   _____

2. Where can you find the table of contents in a book?

   _____

   _____

3. Write a topic that can be found in your book.

   _____

   _____

4. On what page is the topic found?

   _____

Standards and Benchmarks: 4

Researching Lesson 5

Objective

The student will use the computer to gather information on a research topic.

Materials

- computers with Internet access (Having parent helpers in the room for this lesson would be helpful.)
- paper and a pencil for each student

Procedure

1. Schedule a time, if needed, for your students to use the computer lab for researching purposes. (You may need to modify this lesson based on the computer/Internet resources you have available.) Remind students of proper computer lab behavior and procedures before you go.

2. Ahead of time, have computers booted and ready to research on the Internet.

3. Gather students in a group around one computer for a demonstration. Show students how to research and locate information about their animals on the Internet. Walk through this process step by step. Assist students, as needed, in locating information and taking notes.

4. Return to the classroom and discuss their findings as a class. Each student will want a turn to share the latest information they found on the computer. Divide students into groups of four or five. Designate a chair to be the hot seat. Students take turns sitting in the hot seat and sharing with other students the information they gathered. They may use their note taking sheets, as needed. Allow students to ask each other questions after the report has been given. Giving students a chance to share and discuss the information will help clarify for them what they have learned. Have a class discussion about their experience at the computer lab.

5. Schedule more time in the computer lab for students to research, as needed. Be sure to allow plenty of time in your lesson plans for this.

Portfolio Piece

Date the information gathered from the Internet and place it in the students' portfolios. This information can be used at a later time.

Technology Connection

Have students research their animals on the Internet and teach them to print the information and pictures they find.

Assessment

- Check to see that each student has information from the Internet on his or her animal.
- Check off the appropriate research strategy skill (4B) on the Teacher Checklist on page 24 of the Assessment Section. Assess student work using the Research Assessment Rubric on page 52.

Standards and Benchmarks: 1A,4, 4B

Research Learning Center Ideas

Yes/No Sentences

At this center, students will receive practice in reading and extracting information. Have a nonfiction book available at the learning center. Read the book ahead of time. On strips of paper, write down statements about the book. Some of these statements will be information from the book. Some statements will be accurate information about the animal but not in the book, and some statements will be inaccurate statements. Have students read the short nonfiction book. They may read it in pairs or individually. Next, have students take the word strips and place them in one of two piles: "Yes, this information was found in the book," or "No, this information was not from the book." This is a form of both comprehension and note-taking practice for students.

Picture This!

Cut two or three pictures of animals from a colorful magazine and place them along with strips of paper at the center. Put a small box underneath each picture. Students come to this center and look at the pictures. Using the strips of paper, students write a sentence for each picture. (It can be background knowledge, or it can be information they learned just by looking at the picture.) After each student has had a chance to visit this center, read the sentence strips in each box. Share all the information that students wrote for each picture. This is a perfect way to practice note taking using pictures.

Amazing Acrostics

The materials for this center are pieces of paper for each student and crayons. This center will give students a chance to write down things they have researched. Students write the name of their animal vertically down the edge of the paper. Then, for each letter, they will dictate or write a fact about their animal. Next to each fact, they draw a little picture to go with it. Invite students to share their work with classmates.

A Bright Idea

Have newspaper and magazine articles available for each student. These articles need to be written about animals. Have each student read his or her article with a partner. While reading, have students highlight areas of importance with a highlighting pen. Students may choose for themselves what they feel are important sections. Next, have the other student read his or her article with a partner, while marking the selected sections with a highlighting pen. Then have students explain to each other why they highlighted certain portions of the article.

Standards and Benchmarks: 1A, 4, 4B

Home-School Activities

Here are some *optional* research activities that you can do at home. These activities will enrich objectives and lessons being taught in school.

✓ Reporter at Home

Let your child practice being a researcher by studying you! Sit down with your child and come up with a list of questions that he or she could ask you about when you were his or her age. Then have your child ask and record the answers. Encourage the use of complete sentences and punctuation. Read and edit the "report" together offering your child suggestions to improve punctuation, capitalization, and spelling.

✓ Research Across the World

Study a topic together as a family. Perhaps studying a country together could be fun. Go to the local library with your child and look up books about the country selected by your family. Study the culture and traditions of this country. Your family may even have fun with an evening of eating traditional dishes and playing games or other activities from your chosen country.

✓ Hi-Tech Research

Ask questions as a family and research the answers in encyclopedias, on the Internet, or from other resources. Using e-mail, ask questions of friends and family members who also might have information about your questions.

✓ Reading Research

Read articles in the newspaper or in magazines about a selected topic with your child. Discuss what you learn from your research. Express opinions and use your research to back up your ideas.

✓ Research in Action

Make a list of research topics. Discuss with your child the variety of ways that you could get information about each of the topics. Be creative. There are more ways than reading a book to get information. Select one of the topics and plan how to research it. Your child may learn just how easy and fun researching can be.

✓ Panel Discussion

Form a panel of friends and family "experts" on a given topic. Ask questions of each panel member to get answers to your research questions. Let the panel speak and answer questions. Be sure to select a research topic with which each family member or friend has had experience. Take notes on what each panel member says. Make a book of your experiences.

Standards and Benchmarks: 1A, 4, 4B

Research Games

Animal Charades

Students should know quite a bit about the animal that they are studying with the information that they have researched. Have students take turns acting out their animals. See if other students can guess without any hints. Explain and demonstrate how to play charades in the best way possible. Show actions that the animal might make.

Animal Fact-Finding

Have students look over their notes to make sure they can answer many questions about their animals. Then divide the class into groups of four or five. Each student takes a turn being "It." The remaining students in the group ask this person questions about his or her animal that can be answered by *yes* or *no*. Play continues this way until the group guesses the animal. Then, another student takes a turn. Play the game until all students have had a turn.

Race to the Answer

This game will give the students researching and comprehension practice. Ahead of time, select a descriptive paragraph about an animal. (Be sure to pick a paragraph that has lots of information and is written at the level of the students in your class.) Read the paragraph and write questions about the animal on sentence strips. Pair students up with a buddy, pairing good readers with readers that may need more help. Explain that you are going on a research hunt. You are looking for help and you need the students to look for clues. Distribute the paragraph about the animal of your choice. Next, give students time to read the paragraph. Have them look for clues and descriptions about the specific animal. Then hold up the first question word strip. Ask one of the students to point to the part of the paragraph that gives the answer and the other students to raise their hands showing the teacher they are ready. Give all pairs a chance to do this. Once everyone has found the answer, have the first group share the answer aloud. Continue with new questions about the animal.

Research Bingo

Students use the information they gathered from Research Lessons 3 and 4 about the library to play this game. Make blank copies of the Bingo Card on page 51. Fill in the blanks on the card with the names of research materials—computer, encyclopedia, library books, newspaper, etc. Vary the placement of the words on the cards to avoid having all students get bingo simultaneously. (You might hand out blank forms and have the students place the words.) Distribute the different bingo cards to the students. Review each word on the bingo cards. Explain that the first person to get three in a row yells "Research Bingo!" and is the winner. Begin the game by asking questions about where certain information can be found. Students use coins or other markers to cover each space on their Bingo Cards. Use the examples below to help you:

- When I am researching, I have to type on this to get the answers. (computer)
- There are lots of these in the library, but I have to have a library card to use them. (books)
- This comes every day and has lots of words written all over it. (newspaper)
- This big set of books has information in it and is found in ABC order. (encyclopedia)

Standards and Benchmarks: 4

Research Games *(cont.)*

Bingo Card

Research Assessment Rubric

Use the rubric below to assess student progress using researching techniques. The numbers and letters in parenthesis correspond with the Teacher Checklist (page 24) in the Assessment Section.

Competent

The student can independently gather and use information for research purposes. (4)

The student can independently use books to gather information for research purposes. (4B)

The student can independently use a table of contents.

The student can independently examine pictures and charts.

The student can independently use the computer to gather information on a research topic.

Emergent

The student can usually gather and use information for research purposes. (4)

The student can usually use books to gather information for research purposes. (4B)

The student can usually use a table of contents.

The student can usually examine pictures and charts.

The student can usually use the computer to gather information on a research topic.

Beginner

The student requires assistance to gather and use information for research purposes. (4)

The student requires assistance to use books to gather information for research purposes. (4B)

The student requires assistance to use a table of contents.

The student requires assistance to examine pictures and charts.

The student requires assistance to use the computer to gather information on a research topic.

Drafting Your Report

Drafting the report can be difficult for students at this age because they are learning how to write. Students in your classroom will be able to write at a variety of levels. Remember this as you set criteria and expectations for students when they write their drafts. Some lessons give guidelines for what can be expected of students in their writing. Be sure to alter these as needed for your class.

Some students may do better dictating their reports to you, the teacher, or a parent volunteer. Keep in mind that writing for some students may be a barrier to getting the ideas in their heads down on paper.

Standards and Benchmarks: 2A, 3J

Drafting Lesson 1

Objective

The student will use a period after a declarative sentence and a question mark after an interrogative sentence.

Materials

- copy of Telling and Asking Sentences (page 55) for each student
- scissors for each student
- glue for each student

Procedure

1. Write the words *declarative* and *interrogative* on the chalkboard. Explain that a declarative sentence is a telling sentence, while an interrogative sentence is an asking sentence. Discuss the period and the question mark. Have students practice writing periods and question marks in the air.

2. Under the word *declarative*, write a sentence. Share this with the students. Invite students to share declarative sentences. Write them on the chalkboard in the same column as the other declarative sentences. Put emphasis on the periods used at the end of each sentence to demonstrate the appropriate punctuation use.

3. Do this same exercise with the word *interrogative* on the chalkboard. After you have written an example of an interrogative, or asking, sentence, invite students to share some of their own. Once again, place emphasis on the question mark used for these sentences.

4. Send students on a sentence scavenger hunt. Have them locate examples of declarative and interrogative sentences in books, textbooks, posters, signs, newspapers, and other materials found in your classroom.

5. Distribute a copy of Telling and Asking Sentences to each student. Students are to cut and paste sentences under the columns of Telling Sentences and Asking Sentences. Have a completed page of this work sheet available for students to check their work upon completion.

Portfolio Piece

- Have students write letters telling you about their day. Instruct them to include at least two declarative sentences and two interrogative sentences in their letters. Have them place the letters in their portfolios.

- Using a sample in their portfolios from a previous assignment, have students underline samples of declarative and interrogative sentences used in their report writing.

Assessment

- Have students check their work to see if they have completed the work sheet correctly.

- Read through the letters the students write and check to see that two of both declarative and interrogative type sentences were being used.

- Check off the appropriate drafting skills (3J, 2A) on the Teacher Checklist on page 24 of the Assessment Section. Assess student work using the Drafting Assessment Rubric on page 67.

Telling and Asking Sentences

A *declarative sentence* is a telling sentence. It ends with a period. An *interrogative sentence* is an asking sentence. It ends with a question mark. Cut out the sentences below and paste them in the correct column.

Telling Sentences	Asking Sentences

The sky is blue.

They like school.

He is happy.

Where is the book?

What is his name?

How old are they?

How much is it?

Greg talks a lot.

Standards and Benchmarks: 1B, 2A

Drafting Lesson 2

Objective

The student will vary sentence types in his or her report writing.

Materials

- large variety of colored tissue paper available for each student
- piece of colored construction paper for each student
- glue and scissors for each student
- index cards, 4 per student
- model of finished product
- student portfolios

Procedure

1. Prior to teaching this lesson, set up an area in the classroom that will be the designated spot for supplies needed for this project. Keep supplies easily accessible for students. Instruct students that they will be making report projects today about the animals they have been researching. They will also be making models of their animals to accompany their written reports.

2. Hold up the model of a finished product for all students to see. Pass the finished product around the classroom. Ask students to share observations about the project. Write down observations on the chalkboard. As a class, go over the procedure of how to complete this project.

3. Distribute student portfolios so students will have the notes and other information about the animals they researched handy. Distribute four index cards to each child. Each student will be writing a minimum of one sentence on each index card about his or her animal. Review with students, if necessary, the definition of an interrogative and a declarative sentence. Students need to use both declarative and interrogative sentences.

4. Once students have written their sentences on the index cards, have them gather materials needed to make a 3-D model of their animal. (These are "rough" 3-D models that don't need tiny details like eyes, etc.) Students can mold and fold the tissue paper into the shape of their animals. This model will go in the center of the piece of construction paper. An index card will be glued along each edge of the construction paper. Students will need assistance with this project.

Portfolio Piece

Divide students into groups of two or three. Have students share and read their reports to the members of their group. Display the finished products on a bulletin board. Later, save them in the portfolios.

Assessment

- Check to ensure that each student has completed the project as assigned and that there is at least one declarative and interrogative sentence.
- Check off the appropriate drafting skills (1B, 2A) on the Teacher Checklist on pages 23 and 24 of the Assessment Section. Assess student work using the Drafting Assessment Rubric on page 67.

Standards and Benchmarks: 1E, 2A

Drafting Lesson 3

Objective

The student will be able to write a report in logical sequence with a beginning, middle, and end.

Materials

- copy of Sequence Writing (page 58) for each student
- large piece of paper taped to the chalkboard in the front of the classroom (Across the top of the paper, write the words, *First, Then, Next,* and *Finally*.)
- colored markers

Procedure

1. Begin the lesson by sharing an experience you have had. Explain that an experience is easier to understand when the events are placed in sequence or in order. Using your own example, fill in a sentence for each column on your large piece of paper. Under the *First* column, write a sentence describing the first event of your experience. Then move on to the *Then* and *Next* columns. Write another sentence from your experience. Under each column, add more information, adding at least three or more sentences. And under *Finally*, write a concluding sentence about your experience. Reread the sentences, modeling for the students how to write with a logical sequence.

2. Next, ask for volunteers to share experiences. As they share their experiences, fill in their details and sentences on the large piece of paper as they speak. Use a different colored marker than you wrote your experience with so that it is easier for students to denote the two experiences. Encourage the use of the words, *First, Then, Next,* and *Finally* as students share experiences.

3. After you have given plenty of examples on how to fill in the chart, ask for student volunteers to share experiences and to tell you what to write under each column.

4. Next, ask students to think about what they know about their animal. They have had plenty of time to research it and they are ready to share that information. Remind students that telling about their animals in a logical sequence will make it easier for the reader to understand. Model an example of how to fill in the chart on the large piece of paper using information about an animal.

5. Distribute a copy of Sequence Writing to each student. Have students fill in the page using information about the animal they have been researching. As students finish, have them read their information to a partner, using the key words, *First, Then, Next,* and *Finally*.

Portfolio Piece

As students finish the Sequence Writing page, have them place it in their portfolio. This will assist them as they write the rough draft of their research report.

Assessment

- Check to see that students have completed the Sequence Writing page correctly.
- Check off appropriate drafting skills (1E, 2A) on the Teacher Checklist on pages 23 and 24 of the Assessment Section. Assess student work using the Drafting Assessment Rubric on page 67.

Sequence Writing

First . . .

What do you want to share first with the reader? Think of one of the most amazing things about your animal. Share this first.

_____

_____

Then . . .

Write more facts and information that you learned about your animal here.

_____

_____

Next . . .

Write more facts and information that you learned about your animal.

_____

_____

Finally . . .

This is the end of your report. Close with a good finale. Think of something unique you could share about your animal. You may also end your report with a question you still have about your animal.

_____

_____

Standards and Benchmarks: 1E, 2A

Drafting Lesson 4

Objective

The student will be able to write a beginning, middle, and end to a research report.

Materials

- set of index cards available for each group of students
- envelopes
- student portfolios
- copy of page 60, In the Beginning . . ., for each student
- copy of page 61, Drafting Your Report, for each student

Procedure

1. Ahead of time, prepare index card sets for groups of students. On each card, write a sentence from a report you have made up. Each index card represents a part of a report. There needs to be at least five index cards per report. The report parts are a title, an opening sentence, three middle sentences, and a concluding sentence. Place each set of index cards in an envelope for storage. Divide your class into groups of four or five.

2. Explain to students that you have a puzzle for them to solve. Tell them that each envelope contains a report that has been broken up into parts. As a group, have them put the report parts in order. Review each of these parts, as needed.

3. Allow time for the students to put their report parts in order. Circulate the room and help as needed. Encourage students to listen to each other. When students have finished, have one student read the report aloud for the class. Are there any changes that need to be made?

4. Next, ask students what the report would be like if they took a part away. Have students take one index card away. *How is the report different? Why is each of the parts needed for a well-written report?* Discuss the importance of each part.

5. Distribute In the Beginning . . . for students to complete individually. Assist students with reading and writing the sentences correctly.

6. Distribute the Drafting Your Report work sheet to the students. Instruct them to use their notes and the Sequence Writing page in their portfolio for an outline of their draft. Review the guidelines that you will be looking for in their reports. Each report should have a title, an opening sentence, three middle sentences, and a concluding sentence.

Portfolio Piece

When students have completed their rough drafts, divide students into groups of two. Have students read their reports to their partner. Write each of the report parts on the chalkboard. Have students label these parts on their rough drafts. Store the rough drafts in the portfolio. Allow students to take their rough drafts home to get feedback from parents.

Assessment

- Check to see that students completed the page, In the Beginning . . ., correctly.
- Check to see that students have each report part included in their drafts.
- Check off drafting skills (1E, 2A) on the Teacher Checklist on pages 23 and 24 of the Assessment Section. Assess student work using the Drafting Assessment Rubric on page 67.

In the Beginning . . .

Every report has a beginning, a middle, and an end. The beginning interests the reader, the middle gives more information, and the end sums it all up. Read the report parts in the box. Write them in correct order on the lines below.

Dolphins are a lot like humans, and they are just as interesting.

The bottlenose dolphin is the most common dolphin.

The dolphin is a very interesting animal.

Did you know that there are 30–40 dolphin species?

Dolphins are mammals like us.

Dolphins of the Sea

_____
(Title)

_____

_____

_____

_____

_____

_____

_____

_____

Drafting Your Report

_____

(Title)

Standards and Benchmarks: 1B, 1F, 2A

Drafting Lesson 5

Objective

The student will be able to use descriptive words and details in his or her research report.

Materials

- overhead transparency of a descriptive paragraph
- overhead projector
- copy of Descriptive Words (page 63) for each student
- student portfolios
- masking tape

Procedure

1. Place overhead transparency on projector. Ahead of time, cover up adjectives, adverbs, and other descriptive words with masking tape. Read the paragraph to the students without the descriptive words. Discuss how plain the paragraph reads. Discuss with students how their food would taste without spices. Explain that descriptive words are the same way in our writing. Descriptive words make the story better. Read the paragraph again. Ask students to find words that could fit in.

2. Distribute the Descriptive Words page to each student. Go over the directions as a class. Circulate the room to help students as needed. This activity will give students practice in using descriptive words.

3. Have students pull out the rough draft of their report. Direct students to look at their writing. Are there words that students could use or replace to be more descriptive?

4. Divide class into groups of two. As partners, students will read their rough drafts to each other. The listening partner will offer suggestions of descriptive words that could improve the draft. Allow time for both partners to share ideas.

Portfolio

Have students add descriptive words to their rough drafts. Keep this version of the report filed in the student portfolios.

Technology Connection

Teach students how to use the thesaurus on the computer to find other words to replace some of the same words they always use.

Assessment

- Check to see that students have completed the Descriptive Words page correctly.
- Check off drafting skills (1B, 1F, 2A) on the Teacher Checklist on pages 23 and 24 of the Assessment Section. Assess student work using the Drafting Assessment Rubric on page 67.

Standards and Benchmarks: 1B, 1F, 2A

Descriptive Words

Descriptive words give details and information to the reader. Look at the descriptive words in the box.

Add a descriptive word to complete each sentence below.

soft	blue	busy	sweaty	huge

1. The_____box fell off the table.

2. The day was _____.

3. The new house they built was _____.

4. All of the kids came back from recess, and they were _____.

5. The baby kitten was _____.

Write a word that describes each word below.

1. _____recess

2. _____birthday

3. _____apple

4. _____house

5. _____family

6. _____bike

Standards and Benchmarks: 1B, 1E, 1F, 2A, 3H, 3J

Drafting Learning Centers

A Day in the Life of a . . .

This creative writing learning center allows students to share information they have learned about their animals in a creative way. At this center, have a piece of lined paper and a pencil for each student. Across the top of each paper, it should read, "A Day in the Life of a . . ." Each student should finish the sentence by writing the name of the animal he or she has been researching. Students continue on with their paragraphs, writing what a day in the life of the animals they are researching would be like.

The Missing Link

This learning center will help teach logical sequencing in student writing. Cut up construction paper into 3" x 24" (8 cm x 61 cm) strips. On the first strip of paper, each student will write the title of his or her report and staple it together to form a ring. On a second strip of paper, each student will write the introduction, or beginning sentence, for the report. This second strip will be linked through the first ring before stapling it together. Each strip represents a different sentence of the report. Students will continue attaching strips in this fashion until all sentences of their reports have been written and added to the chain.

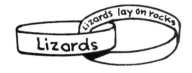
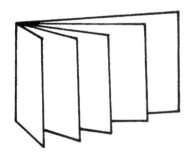

Flip Books

To make a flip book, take three pieces of paper and place them on top of each other. Slide the first page up approximately one inch (2.54 cm), and do this with each piece of paper. Then fold the pages forward to create six graduated layers. Each paper will stick out approximately one inch (2.54 cm) from the bottom. Staple the pages at the fold. Then have students write a different sentence about their research animals on each page. Have crayons available for students to illustrate their sentences. Use the front page as the title page and have students write the name of their research animals as well as their own names.

Research Charades

Provide strips of paper at this learning center. As students come to the center, they are to write sentences about their animals doing something on the strips. (Reviewing verbs and action words before this center might be necessary.) Place all of the strips of paper in a bowl. Each student then draws a slip of paper out and acts out what the sentence says the animal is doing. The other students at the center guess what animal the student is acting out.

Facts and Opinions

Have strips of white paper available for your students at this center. Thinking about their research animal, each student writes down at least three facts and three opinions about the animal. Place the strips of paper in a bowl or other container. As a group, students draw a strip of paper from the bowl and determine whether they think it is either fact or opinion. At the end of the day, you could do this again as a whole class.

Standards and Benchmarks: 1B, 1E, 1F, 2A, 3H, 3J

Home-School Activities

Here are some *optional* drafting activities that you can do at home. These activities will enrich objectives and lessons being taught in school.

✓ Show and Tell

Your child will be bringing home the rough draft report that he or she has written about the animal he or she is researching. Set aside some quiet time to let your child share this draft with you. Read it together and ask questions about the animal he or she researched. Provide positive feedback for your child's writing abilities and progress.

✓ Expert for a Day

Set aside a place at the table for an expert to visit your family. Tell the family that you have invited an expert on a specific animal to come and share information with the family. Decorate a place mat or make a sign designating your child as the expert. Let your child share the research information with the family and allow family members to ask questions. You may even make this a special night and invite special friends or family members to participate.

✓ Write a Letter

After discussing and sharing in the excitement of learning with your child, have your child write a letter to someone far away about the animal he or she researched. Have colored paper, stickers, markers, crayons, or other materials available to make a nice card or letter. Have your child share all the information he or she has learned in the letter.

✓ Using Your Senses

Talk with your child about the senses of sight, sound, smell, taste, and touch. Ask your child what the animal experiences with these senses. Is there one sense that this animal relies upon heavily? How does the animal use its senses for safety, protection, finding food, adventure, mobility, etc.

✓ Dramatize It

Encourage your child to create a skit about his or her research animal. Help with costumes, as needed. Your child could invite friends or family members to participate in the skit. Plan a time for your child to perform the play with friends and family as the audience. It doesn't take much time to throw something together with your child using his or her imagination.

Standards and Benchmarks: 1B, 1E, 1F, 2A, 3H, 3J

Drafting Games

Descriptive Details

This game will reinforce describing with details. Divide your class into small groups. Each student writes the name of his or her research animal on a strip of paper. Place all of the strips in a pile. The first player begins the game by drawing an animal strip and saying, "The (fill in the name of the animal) is (fill in a descriptive word or detail about the animal.)" The next player repeats the sentence and ends it with a different detail. Keep going around the group until everyone has had a turn to say a detail about the animal. The next player draws an animal and the game continues on as before.

Sequence Memory Game

This game is sure to give students sequencing practice. Divide students into small groups. Give each student three index cards. On the index cards, each student draws a different picture of his or her animal doing something in sequence. The index cards will represent what happens first, second, and last. Shuffle all the cards and place them face down in the center of the group. The first player draws three cards. If they are part of the same group, the player takes them and places them in sequence. If he or she can get them in the right order, then he or she gets a point. If the cards are not part of the same grouping, they are turned back over and another student gets a turn. The player with the most cards, in sequence, wins.

Fishing for Animals

Divide your class into small groups. Give each player six index cards. On three index cards, each player writes the name of his or her animal. On the other three cards, he or she writes one fact on each card about his or her animal. Shuffle all the cards together as a group. The first player deals four cards to each student. Place the remaining cards in a pile. Students try to match up the animals with correct facts about the animal. They ask each other for cards and take a card off the pile if they did not get a card from the group. The winner is the player with the most matches of the animals with their facts.

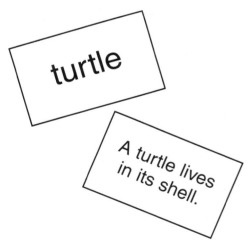

Super Sentences

Divide your class into small groups for this game. Explain that they will be using index cards to write sentences about animals. Write a word for a possible sentence on each index card. Get your information from the rough drafts that your students have written. Keep the sentence ideas simple. Each sentence should have cards for a noun, a verb, an adjective, or an adverb, and a question mark or period. Remind students to remember punctuation. Shuffle all the cards together. Have one student deal all the cards to the players. Players read the cards they get and try to make sentences with them. Students may trade cards, as needed, to make sentences. Have students check each others' sentences to make sure that they are correct. (As a variation of this game, you could have students write their own sentences using more index cards.)

66

Drafting Assessment Rubric

Use the rubric below to assess student progress using drafting skills. The numbers and letters in parenthesis correspond with the Teacher Checklist (pages 23 and 24) in the Assessment Section.

Competent

The student can independently use strategies to draft and revise written work. (1B)

The student can independently reread written work for meaning.

The student can independently vary sentence types.

The student can independently add descriptive words and details.

The student can independently incorporate suggestions from peers and teachers.

The student can independently sharpen the focus.

The student can independently dictate or write with a logical sequence of events. (1E)

The student can independently use general, frequently used words to convey basic ideas. (2A)

The student can independently dictate or write detailed descriptions of familiar persons, places, objects, or experiences. (1F)

Emergent

The student can usually use strategies to draft and revise written work. (1B)

The student can usually reread written work for meaning.

The student can usually vary sentence types.

The student can usually add descriptive words and details.

The student can usually incorporate suggestions from peers and teachers.

The student can usually sharpen the focus.

The student can usually dictate or write with a logical sequence of events. (1E)

The student can usually use general, frequently used words to convey basic ideas. (2A)

The student can usually dictate or write detailed descriptions of familiar persons, places, objects, or experiences. (1F)

Beginner

The student requires assistance to use strategies to draft and revise written work. (1B)

The student requires assistance to reread written work for meaning.

The student requires assistance to vary sentence types.

The student requires assistance to add descriptive words and details.

The student requires assistance to incorporate suggestions from peers and teachers.

The student requires assistance to sharpen the focus.

The student requires assistance to dictate or write with a logical sequence of events. (1E)

The student requires assistance to use general, frequently used words to convey basic ideas. (2A)

The student requires assistance to dictate or write detailed descriptions of familiar persons, places, objects, or experiences. (1F)

Editing and Revising Your Report

This next section will enable students to edit and revise the drafts of their reports. Students will also be editing the reports of other students in the class. Being able to edit and revise is a high level skill in the report writing process. Editing and revising requires being able to see the big picture and understand concepts of grammar, punctuation, capitalization, and spelling.

Adjusting the expectations for the students in your class may include things such as having beginning writers edit just for capital letters in the beginning of the sentence or having emergent writers edit for capitalization at the beginning of sentences and punctuation at the end of sentences. Competent writers can be expected to edit for punctuation, capitalization, and begin editing for spelling errors. Be sure to keep the editing at the level of each student. Increase the expectation as student progress dictates.

Standards and Benchmarks: 1C

Editing Lesson 1

Objective

The student will be able to edit for grammar, punctuation, and spelling at an appropriate developmental level.

Keep in mind that all students are at different levels. You may select one area (capitalization, punctuation, or spelling) for students to focus on in their editing and add areas as students progress.

Materials

- enlarged version of Proofreading Chart (page 70) to display in the classroom
- copy of page 70, Proofreading Chart, for each student
- transparency of page 71, Sample Reports for Editing, and an overhead projector
- copy of page 72, Editing Practice, for each student

Procedure

1. Explain to students that when we write, we often make mistakes in our writing that need correction. Each time we write something, we should reread it to make sure that there aren't any mistakes in our writing. Display the enlarged Proofreading Chart for the students. Go through the chart and show students each of the errors commonly made and the symbols used to show the corrections needed. Have students practice making each symbol in the air or on a piece of paper to show the mistake. Do this for different types of errors.

2. Now, place the transparency of the Sample Reports for Editing on the overhead projector. Tell students that you will be correcting them together as a class. Distribute the copies of the Proofreading Chart for the students. Review once more the types of mistakes and the symbols used for these mistakes. Read the reports. Have students raise their hands when they see a mistake that was made. Make the symbol directly on the transparency for all students to see. Follow this same procedure sentence by sentence. At the end, direct students' attention to any errors they may have missed and add the symbols.

3. Distribute the copies of Editing Practice to the students. Have students read each sentence, look for mistakes, and correct the mistakes by rewriting the sentence correctly. When students have finished, have them share their pages with a buddy sitting next to them, and discuss what each student wrote.

Portfolio Piece

Direct students to place the Proofreading Chart in their portfolios for future reference.

Assessment

- As students complete the Editing Practice page, circulate around the room to see that students have done it correctly.
- Check off the appropriate editing skill (1C) on the Teacher Checklist on page 23 of the Assessment Section. Assess student work using the Editing and Revising Assessment Rubric on page 85.

Proofreading Chart

Use these proofreading marks to show where changes need to be made in report writing.

Take out something.		The big boy ~~boy~~ yelled.
Add a comma.		We ate carrots, peas, and pears.
Add a period.	⊙	The bat flew into the cave.
Begin a new paragraph.	¶	¶I have a pet dog. His name is Duke. He is brown and has big eyes. I also have a cat.
Make a capital letter.	≡	sam is nine today.
Make a lower case letter.	/ lc	Today is her Birthday.
Word is spelled wrong.	◯ sp	Jumpas high as you can.

Read the sample report below with the editing marks to see how to use them.

my shoes

¶i got up this morning and i couldn't find my ~~shoes~~ shoes. i

looked in the car, the hall, and under my bed. i couldn't

find them anywhere. then my mom told me to check in

the shoe basket. Tehy were there! I couln't believe it.

now i am Ready to go to schol.

Sample Reports for Editing

There are some mistakes in these reports. Can you find the mistakes?
Use the editing marks to show the mistakes.

---

meadow monkeys

in the meadow you will find many animals one of these animals is
called the harvest mouse this tiny animal can climb from one
plant to another and look just like a Monkey harvest mice climb
these Plants looking fore food they eat as much as they can in the
summer for winter the harvest Mouse scampers through the
meadow along with all the other animals

---

snake in the grass

snakes are some of the scariest animals the european grass
snake is not poisonous, but they can make an awful smell to scare
enemies away the grass snake likes to lay in the sun grass
snakes eat frogs and newts they live in marshy meadows
sometimes the the grass sanke will pretend to be Dead The more
you learn about snakes, the less scary they are

Editing Practice

Use the proofreading marks to correct these sentences. Then write each sentence correctly.

1. dolphins is good swimmers

   _____

2. are lions cats and tigers from the same same family

   _____

3. many bugs buzz and fli around

   _____

4. do turtles and fish eat them

   _____

5. their are many animals that we cant see

   _____

6. dolphins are mammals just like Us

   _____

Standards and Benchmarks: 1C, 3H

Editing Lesson 2

Objective

The student will be able to use a dictionary and other resources to spell words.

Materials

- age-appropriate dictionaries for students
- student portfolios

Procedure

1. Discuss with students the different places that they can go to find out how to spell a word correctly. Some suggestions might include the following: ask a friend, ask your teacher or other adult, look in a dictionary, use a computer spell check, etc.

2. Distribute age-appropriate dictionaries for students. Allow time for students to look through the dictionaries. Discuss what can be found in a dictionary. *What information does a dictionary tell you? What is hard about using a dictionary?* Discuss with your class strategies to use when working with a dictionary.

3. Pair students up with partners, and have them get the rough draft copy of the animal report with the proofreading symbols on it from the previous lesson out of their portfolios. The proofreading symbols will show students the things that need to be changed. The words that are misspelled in the report have been circled. Have students look up all of the misspelled words in a dictionary. Working with a partner can be helpful when locating the words in a dictionary.

4. Once students have located the correct spelling for the word, have them write the correct version above the misspelling in their reports.

Portfolio Piece

Have students keep the rough drafts with spelling corrections filed in their portfolios. They will be using them in Lesson 5 when they rewrite their rough drafts.

Assessment

- Circulate around the room to see that students are using the dictionary to correct their spelling errors. You may need to alter the assignment for some students in your classroom.

- Check off the appropriate drafting skills (1C, 3H) on the Teacher Checklist on pages 23 and 24 of the Assessment Section. Assess student work using the Editing and Revising Assessment Rubric on page 85.

Standards and Benchmarks: 3J

Editing Lesson 3

Objective

The student will be able to use periods, question marks, and commas in his or her writing.

Materials

- copy of page 75, Punctuation Please, for each student
- portfolios available for students

Procedure

1. Write a paragraph without any punctuation marks on the chalkboard before students arrive in the classroom. Ask students to read the paragraph. Ask them if they can figure out what is missing. Explain how important punctuation is in our writing, and yet punctuation errors are very common.

2. Discuss how punctuation marks put pauses or breaks in our writing and tell a reader when he or she is at the end of a thought. Without punctuation marks, thoughts and ideas would run together, and it would be difficult to understand writing.

3. Distribute a copy of Punctuation Please to each student. Have them work independently to complete this page. When students are finished, go over it together as a class. Be sure that students check their own work to make sure they are correcting any mistakes they made.

4. Next, divide students into groups of two or three. Have students take turns writing a sentence that has no punctuation marks in it. The remaining students add the needed punctuation marks. Have the first student be the teacher and check the sentences and punctuation to make sure they are correct.

Portfolio Piece

Have students check their rough draft of their research report and look to make sure that punctuation marks are being used correctly. Allow time for students to correct their punctuation as needed.

Assessment

- Check to make sure that students have completed the Punctuation Please page correctly.
- Check off drafting skill (3J) on the Teacher Checklist on page 24 of the Assessment Section. Assess student work using the Editing and Revising Assessment Rubric on page 85.

Punctuation Please

Write a telling sentence about a spider spinning a web. Be sure to put a period at the end.

_____

_____

Write an asking question about a spider catching a fly. Be sure to put a question mark at the end.

_____

_____

The spider makes a web to catch its prey. Look at the word web below. Read the words in the web. Write a telling sentence and a question using the words that are joined together. Look at the samples. Write your sentences below and be sure to check your punctuation.

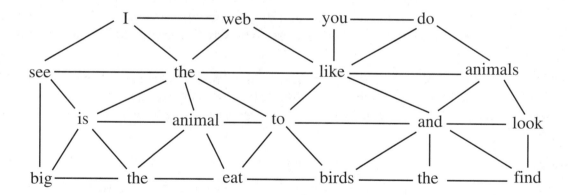

Sample Telling Sentences:
The animal is big.
I see the animal.

Sample Questions:
Do you like the web?
Do you like to eat?

_____

_____

_____

_____

Standards and Benchmarks: 1D

Editing Lesson 4

Objective

The student will be able to help classmates apply grammatical and mechanical conventions and spell frequently used words correctly.

Materials

- copy of page 77, Peer Response Work Sheet, for each student

- student portfolios

Procedure

1. Tell students that getting feedback from others improves our writing. Other people can see things in our writing that we are missing, and they can offer good suggestions. Have each student take out his or her report draft. Put each student with a partner. Be sure they have not read each other's report drafts yet. Have students read through each other's reports and add proofreading marks to any errors. When completed, have student partners work together to make the necessary changes.

2. Next, distribute copies of the Peer Response Work Sheet for the students. Go over this page together as a class. Read each of the questions and discuss possible answers. Show students what their job will be as they review their partner's report. Allow time for students to complete the peer response.

3. Have students exchange papers to read the critiques of their research reports. Have a discussion as a class. Some of the questions might include the following suggestions: *Did your partner have some good ideas? What can you change in your report to make it better? What do you need to do now?*

Portfolio Piece

Have students make any needed changes to their rough drafts. Place the rough drafts back in their portfolios when completed. Place the Peer Response pages in their portfolios as well.

Assessment

- Check to see that students have completed the Peer Response page. Answers will vary. Some students will need more help filling this form out than others.

- Check off editing skill (1D) on the Teacher Checklist on page 23 of the Assessment Section. Assess student work using the Editing and Revising Assessment Rubric on page 85.

Peer Response Work Sheet

Your Name: _____

Author's Name: _____

Circle the answer to these statements.

1. This report is interesting.	very much	somewhat
2. This report made sense to me.	very much	somewhat
3. The report is clearly written.	very much	somewhat

Finish the following statements as best you can. Remember your job is to help the writer.

1. One thing I really like about this report is . . .

_____

_____

2. One thing I think would make the report better is . . .

_____

_____

3. Something I would like the author to tell more about is . . .

_____

_____

4. My other comment is . . .

_____

_____

Standards and Benchmarks: 1B, 1D

Editing and Revising Lesson 5

Objective

The student will be able to ask questions and receive feedback about his or her report writing.

Materials

- copy of page 79, Editing and Revising, for each student
- portfolios available for students
- copy of page 80, Revising Your Report, for each student

Procedure

1. Have students pull out the rough draft copies of their own reports from their portfolios. Using the Proofreading Charts in their portfolios, have students edit their own reports, using the symbols to show where corrections are needed.

2. Next, distribute the copies of the Editing and Revising work sheet to the students. Go over each of the questions together as a class. Allow students time to ask questions. They will be asking questions and making comments about their own writing. Read each question or sentence on the Editing and Revising page and have students answer them as you read them.

3. Instruct students to then look at their answers to these questions and make changes to the rough draft copy of their research reports. Are there areas that need fixing?

4. As students work on this task, invite students to come up one at a time for a teacher/student conference. At this conference, have students read their reports to you. Read through the editing questions. Offer suggestions and help as needed. Show students how to make changes if they are unclear. Help them delete information from their reports that does not fit in. Clear, specific suggestions and instructions are needed at this point. Students will be rewriting their drafts and need to know the information that will help them be successful at this point in the process.

Portfolio Piece

Have students rewrite and revise their drafts on the Revising Your Report work sheet provided on page 80. File this in the student portfolio for later use.

Assessment

- As students complete the Editing and Revising page, circulate around the room to see that students have done it correctly. You may need to alter the assignment for some students in your classroom.

- Check off drafting skills (1B, 1D) on the Teacher Checklist on page 23 of the Assessment Section. Assess student work using the Editing and Revising Assessment Rubric on page 85.

Editing and Revising

Now that you have finished writing the draft copy of your report, read through it one more time. Ask yourself these questions and fill in the apple if the answer is yes.

1. Does my report have a title?

2. Does my report have an interesting beginning?

3. Are there at least five sentences in my report?

4. Is my report written clearly, and does it make sense?

5. Is there a good ending to my report?

6. Are all of the words spelled correctly?

7. Did I punctuate correctly?

8. Do I have capital letters in the right places?

9. Is my report written neatly so others can read it?

10. Does my report have all the necessary information?

Revising Your Report

_____

(Title)

_____

_____

_____

_____

_____

_____

_____

_____

_____

_____

_____

_____

_____

_____

_____

_____

_____

_____

_____

_____

_____

_____

Standards and Benchmarks: 1B, 1C, 1D, 2A, 3H, 3J

Editing and Revising Learning Centers

Pass It On Reports

As students come to this center, have copies of page 82, Animals Can Be Fun, available for each student. Each student begins writing the first sentence of this group report stating why animals can be fun. After a few minutes, each student takes his or her paper and passes it to the right, rotating each report to the next student. Students begin writing another sentence or completing the previous sentence on the new page. Keep rotating the reports until all students have had a turn to add to each other's original papers. Return the papers to the original owner. Have each student take a turn sharing the group animal report. Finally, have students work as a group to edit each report, using the symbols from the Proofreading Chart on page 70.

Sentence Savvy

Write sentences on strips of paper. Make errors of capitalization, punctuation, or spelling on each sentence strip. Place the sentence strips in a bowl. When students come to this learning center, they are to draw sentences from the bowl and make corrections on a piece of paper.

Picture This!

Gather a collection of pictures from magazines and store advertisements. Place the pictures in a box or other container. Have students draw a picture from the box and write a sentence about it. Have students check and edit each others' sentences for punctuation, capitalization, and spelling. When finished, have students draw another picture from the box and go through the same procedure.

Nuts About Noodles

Have alphabet noodles and elbow macaroni available at this learning center. Have students write sentences about their animal using the noodles and macaroni. The elbow macaroni can be used for commas and contractions. Students glue the noodles onto a piece of construction paper and add letters, etc., as needed with a marker.

Four Square

Fold a piece of paper into fourths. At the top of each fourth, write a different punctuation mark/capital letter. Using old newspapers and magazines, have students cut out examples of each of these punctuation marks and capitals, and paste them in the correct square. (See the example to the right.)

?	.
capital letter	,

Animals Can Be Fun

Write your group report below, and then edit your report together.

Standards and Benchmarks: 1B, 1C, 1D, 2A, 3H, 3J

Home-School Activities

Here are some *optional* editing and revising activities that you can do at home. These activities will enrich objectives and lessons being taught in school.

✓ Dictionary Fun

Pull out the dictionary at your house and spend an evening perusing it with your child. Just look at different words that can be found in the dictionary. Allow your child time to ask questions and make observations about different words in the dictionary. Encourage your child to think of a word that he or she would like to look up. Assist him or her in finding the word in the dictionary. Read together the definition or definitions and show him or her where the pronunciation of each word can be found.

✓ Punctuation Fun

Write a period, a question mark, and a comma on separate pieces of paper or index cards. More than one card can be made for each punctuation mark. Place the cards in a pile. Family members draw a card and have to say a sentence that would use this punctuation mark in it.

✓ Dictionary Definitions

Play this game as a family with a dictionary. Have a family member look up a word. He or she then says three definitions of this word (two that are fictitious and one that is the true definition). The other family members have to guess which one is the right definition. A point is given to each person who guesses the right definition. The person with the most points at the end of the game wins. For families with young children, form teams with an adult or older child.

✓ Newspaper Highlights

Give your child a highlighter marker and an old newspaper or magazine. Using the marker, have your child highlight when a capital letter has been used. Review with your child the times when a capital letter is needed. (At the beginning of a sentence, a title, a person's name, the date, etc.)

✓ ABC Throughout the House

Write each letter of the alphabet on a piece of paper. Have your child go throughout the house and find items that begin with that letter. See if your child can find an item that begins with each letter of the alphabet.

✓ Reading Review

Each time you read a story to your child, ask him or her to look for punctuation, capitalization, or spelling words. This will heighten your child's awareness of these concepts.

Standards and Benchmarks: 1B, 1C, 1D, 2A, 3H

Editing and Revising Games

To the End

This game is similar to the game of football. Divide your class into two teams. Have students write down five sentences each, but have them leave off the end punctuation marks. Designate certain areas of the classroom as the 50-yard line, 40-yard line, etc. Choose a quarterback from each team to read the sentences aloud to the other team. The quarterback from Team A reads the sentences to Team B. The first player suggests what the correct punctuation should be. If he or she answers correctly, the "ball" is moved to the 40-yard line. Play continues in this fashion until a touchdown is made. Then the opposing team gets a chance to make a touchdown using the same procedure. If the wrong punctuation mark is given, it is the other team's turn.

If space does not allow for students to move around the room, make a game board for the wall. Draw a football field on a large piece of paper, marking the field every ten yards. At one end of the field, write Touchdown Team A! At the other end of the field, write Touchdown Team B! Display the field on a magnetic board. Create a football magnet and allow the student who guesses correctly to move the magnet when he or she correctly names the punctuation.

Words Inside of Words

This game will get kids thinking. Each student needs a piece of scrap paper and a pencil. Write a word on the chalkboard. Make it a fairly long word with many letters. The students then write down as many words as they can think of that use letters from that word. After a minute, have students put their pencils down. Students receive one point for every word that they wrote down. Students get an additional point for each word they wrote down that is spelled correctly. Play continues with a new word.

Spelling Bee

Ask each student to make a list of words about his or her animal that will be part of the spelling bee. This will give students input on the words they have to spell. Gather all of the word lists. Line students across the front of the classroom. Ask each student to spell a word from his or her own word list. If they get it correct, they can keep standing. If they spell it incorrectly, they must sit down. The last student standing is the winner.

Spelling Baseball

Set up your classroom in the shape of a baseball diamond, using a chair for home, first, second, and third base. Divide your class into two teams. The first team goes into the "outfield." The other team forms a line behind home plate. The teacher is the pitcher. Read off a word to the first batter. If the batter spells it correctly, he or she advances to first base and continues to move with each subsequent correct spelling. If a batter spells a word wrong, he or she strikes out. Points are awarded to a team when the players make it to home base. Play continues until each student on both teams has had a chance to "bat."

Editing & Revising Assessment Rubric

Use the rubric below to assess student progress using editing and revising skills. The numbers and letters in parenthesis correspond with the Teacher Checklist (pages 23 and 24) in the Assessment Section.

Competent

The student can independently use strategies to draft and revise written work. (1B)

The student can independently reread written work for meaning.

The student can independently delete extraneous information.

The student can independently rearrange words, sentences, and paragraphs to improve meaning.

The student can independently incorporate suggestions from peers and teachers.

The student can independently use strategies to edit and publish written work. (1C)

The student can independently proofread using a dictionary and other resources.

The student can independently edit for grammar, punctuation, capitalization, and spelling.

The student can independently ask questions and make comments about writing. (1D)

The student can independently help classmates apply grammatical and mechanical conventions.

The student can independently use conventions of spelling in written compositions. (3H)

Emergent

The student can usually use strategies to draft and revise written work. (1B)

The student can usually reread written work for meaning.

The student can usually delete extraneous information.

The student can usually rearrange words, sentences, and paragraphs to improve meaning.

The student can usually incorporate suggestions from peers and teachers.

The student can usually use strategies to edit and publish written work. (1C)

The student can usually proofread using a dictionary and other resources.

The student can usually edit for grammar, punctuation, capitalization, and spelling.

The student can usually ask questions and make comments about writing. (1D)

The student can usually help classmates apply grammatical and mechanical conventions.

The student can usually use conventions of spelling in written compositions. (3H)

Beginner

The student requires assistance to use strategies to draft and revise written work. (1B)

The student requires assistance to reread written work for meaning.

The student requires assistance to delete extraneous information.

The student requires assistance to rearrange words, sentences, and paragraphs to improve meaning.

The student requires assistance to incorporate suggestions from peers and teachers.

The student requires assistance to use strategies to edit and publish written work. (1C)

The student requires assistance to proofread using a dictionary and other resources.

The student requires assistance to edit for grammar, punctuation, capitalization, and spelling.

The student requires assistance to ask questions and make comments about writing. (1D)

The student requires assistance to help classmates apply grammatical and mechanical conventions.

The student requires assistance to use conventions of spelling in written compositions. (3H)

Publishing Your Report

Publishing the report is the final step of the writing process. Students have gone through many steps to reach this point. Using a variety of formats to publish and share the report can be fun and interesting for the students.

There are lessons in this section for using the computer to write the final draft. Parent volunteers will be very helpful at this stage. Students at this level may need help with using the keyboard to type, space words, make capital letters, and indent, but given a few opportunities for practice, you will be surprised how quickly students can word process. Some students will be ready to use the spell check. Be sure to adjust the expectations of this activity for individuals.

Computers also lend themselves to editing and revising easily. Teach students how to use graphics and print, if desired.

Standards and Benchmarks: 1C

Publishing Lesson 1

Objective

The student will be able to write a finished product.

Materials

- computer/printer access for each child
- student portfolios
- copy of page 88, Report Writing Questionnaire, for each student

Procedure

1. Have students locate the edited rough draft of their animal reports in their portfolios. Instruct students to read through these edited reports one more time. Are there any last minute changes? Are capitals, punctuation marks, and spelling errors corrected? Explain to students that they are at the point where they will be writing a finished product of their animal reports. They will be using a computer to word process these reports. (If no computers are available, have students write the final draft.)

2. Make arrangements for students to use the computers. Explain to students what a heading on a report is. Have students write their names and the date as their heading. Next on the report should be the title. You may need to help students with centering. Show the options of enlarging and bolding the title to your students. You may also need to show students how to make a capital letter on the keyboard.

3. Next, have students begin typing their reports. When completed, have them double check spelling and punctuation of their typed version with the edited version. Assist students with spacing and any other areas of concern.

4. Help students save their work in a file and print the finished products. Allow students time to share their finished products with partners. This is an exciting stage in the report writing process.

Portfolio Piece

Print a copy of the reports for students to include in their portfolios. Spend time as a class allowing students to look through their portfolios to see the progress and growth they have made over the last few weeks. Have students locate the following documents: brainstorming web page, research notes taken from books and other resources in the library, rough draft of animal report, edited version of the rough draft, and then the typed final draft. Arrange these papers in order. Discuss with students how this is a process.

Have students write a reflection of how they feel about the process. How did they improve? What did they learn? Have students complete the Report Writing Questionnaire and place it in their portfolios along with the set of papers representing the report writing process. You may need to go over each segment of the report writing process.

Assessment

- Check off the appropriate publishing skill (1C) on the Teacher Checklist on page 23 of the Assessment Section. Assess student work using the Publishing Assessment Rubric on page 97.

Report Writing Questionnaire

Now that you have completed the report writing process, answer the following questions.

1. What did you learn as you completed each part of the report writing process?

   ✮ Brainstorming _____

   _____

   ✮ Researching _____

   _____

   ✮ Drafting Your Report _____

   _____

   ✮ Editing and Revising Your Report _____

   _____

   ✮ Publishing Your Report _____

   _____

2. What was your favorite part about writing a report? _____

   _____

3. What did you learn from writing this report? _____

   _____

4. What questions do you still have about your animal? _____

   _____

Standards and Benchmarks: 1C

Publishing Lesson 2

Objective

The student will be able to incorporate illustrations into his or her report.

Materials

- lined paper with space at the top for illustrations (enough to make a book for each student)
- white construction paper for each student
- crayons or colored pencils for each student
- watercolor paints and brushes for each student

Procedure

1. In this activity, students will be making a book with the report. Make a book for each student by stapling lined paper inside a white piece of construction paper. On each page of the book, students will be writing one sentence from their report and illustrating this page with crayons or colored pencils. Be sure to include a title page for each student to write the title and his or her name as the author.

2. After students have completed writing and illustrating their reports, distribute watercolor paints and other materials needed to paint the covers of the books. If needed, have each student draw a sketch of the animal on another piece of paper as practice. Allow time for the covers to dry.

3. Divide students into groups of four or five. Have each student take a turn reading his or her book to the other members of the group. Place these books in your classroom library for students to read and enjoy.

Portfolio Piece

On the inside cover, have students write a dedication. Explain to the students that the dedication is to thank or acknowledge someone special. As an optional activity, you could also take a picture of the author or write a few sentences about him or her to place on the inside cover under the dedication.

Technology Connection

Students could type their reports on different pages that can be folded into a book. Encourage students to use spell check on the computer. When completed, have students print their pages and staple them into books.

Assessment

Check off the appropriate publishing skill (1C) on the Teacher Checklist on page 23 of the Assessment Section. Assess student work using the Publishing Assessment Rubric on page 97.

Standards and Benchmarks: 1H

Publishing Lesson 3

Objective
The student will be able to write in a variety of formats.

Materials
- copy of page 91, Publishing Poetry, for each student
- lined pieces of paper for each student
- pieces of white construction paper for each student
- crayons and colored pencils for each student

Procedure
1. There are many different ways to write a poem. Now that students are loaded with information about their research animals, have them write poems with this information. Teach about one type of poem at a time. Distribute a copy of Publishing Poetry to the students. Give instructions for each type of poem.

The Acrostic Poem
Each student writes the name of his or her animal down the left side of the paper. For each letter of the animal, the student writes a describing word or phrase about the animal.

The Shape Poem
Shape poetry can be fun. Words are written around the outline of the shape of the student's animal. The shape of the animal can be traced and then cut out to use as a guide.

The Diamante Poem
This poem uses a lot of describing and action words. All of these words are about the student's animal. Use the guide on the following page.

---

2. Have students write each type of poetry on a piece of lined paper. After completing the poems, have students edit them and check for punctuation, capitalization, and spelling errors. When students have proofread their poems, have them make the final draft of each poem on the piece of white construction paper.

Portfolio Piece
Have students select one of the poems they wrote to place in their portfolios.

Assessment
- Check to see that students have completed the poems in the correct format.
- Check off the appropriate publishing skill (1H) on the Teacher Checklist on page 23 of the Assessment Section. Assess student work using the Publishing Assessment Rubric on page 97.

Publishing Poetry

There many different ways to write a poem. Look at the samples below for ideas.

Acrostic Poems

Write the name of your animal down the left side of the paper. For each letter in the name, write a describing word or phrase about your animal.

All kinds
Names for all of them
Interesting
Most make sound
Amazing
Live in habitats
Search for food

Shape Poems

Shape poetry can be fun. Words are written around the outline of the shape of your animal. The shape of your animal can be traced and then cut out to use as a guide.

Diamante Poems

This poem uses a lot of describing and action words. All of these words are about your animal. Use the guide below.

Line 1: Name of your animal
Line 2: Two describing words
Line 3: Three action words
Line 4: A four-word phrase
Line 5: Three action words
Line 6: Two describing words
Line 7: Name of your animal again

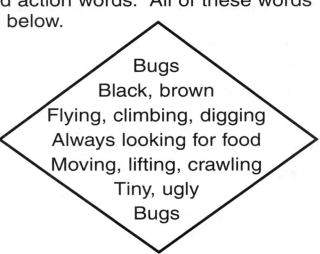

Bugs
Black, brown
Flying, climbing, digging
Always looking for food
Moving, lifting, crawling
Tiny, ugly
Bugs

Standards and Benchmarks: 1H

Publishing Lesson 4

This lesson is to be done in preparation for Publishing Lesson 5.

Objective

The student will be able to write in a variety of formats.

Materials

- poster board for each student
- markers, colored pencils, or crayons for each student
- samples of advertisements
- stencils, stickers, construction paper, magazines for pictures, etc.
- glue or glue sticks for students

Procedure

1. Distribute poster board to each student. Students will be making advertising posters about their animals. Show samples of advertisements and discuss with students how to make their posters interesting and inviting.

2. Tell students to think about the following questions before making their posters: *What is the purpose of the poster? Who is my audience?* Go over the following poster-making guidelines with your students:

    Words: The main idea is the attention-getting message of the poster. The main idea should be in big letters. Detail information is usually in smaller letters and can be separated by "bullets." Bullets are dots or dashes at the beginning of a short phrase.

    Pictures: Art is used on a poster to get attention, to make the poster more attractive, to demonstrate the message, or to help explain a concept. For your poster you may use pictures cut from magazines, photographs, or your own drawings and illustrations (draw in pencil first). You may wish to use boxes or decorative borders to organize your words and pictures.

    Lettering: Always use pencil first when making handwritten letters. If you use a stencil for letters, make light pencil lines to use as a guide. When using cutout letters, position them on your poster first. When you are sure they will fit, glue them down.

3. Distribute materials for students to make their advertising posters of their animals. Anything that you have available for students to use would be helpful.

4. Allow time to work on the posters. Circulate and assist where necessary.

Portfolio Piece

Have students write reflections about how well they did on their posters. *What are the good points about the poster? Is the poster a neat and attractive display?* Get posters ready to display for Publishing Lesson 5 on page 93.

Assessment

- Check to see that students have completed the poster assignment completely.
- Check off the appropriate publishing skill (1H) on the Teacher Checklist on page 23 of the Assessment Section. Assess student work using the Publishing Assessment Rubric on page 97.

Standards and Benchmarks: 1C

Publishing Lesson 5

Objective

The student will be able to share the finished product.

Materials

- advertising posters made by students
- final printed copy of research report
- other materials made in various units that can be displayed at student desks

Procedure

1. Invite other classes in your school to come to your class for Ask the Expert Day. Ask the Expert Day is an opportunity for your students to share their finished products and projects of their report writing. This is an appropriate time for students to also share the information they have gathered in a variety of formats.

2. Prior to classes coming to your classroom, arrange student desks in a u-shape so that it will be easy for guests to move throughout the classroom. At each desk, students will exhibit their posters, their final reports, and any other projects they wish to share, such as their clay animals, the animal poetry, the animal books, etc. Anything done up to this point of the unit can be on display.

3. Explain to students that they are the *experts for the day* on the animals that they have been researching over the last few weeks. Assist students in setting up their displays. Explain to students that other classes will be coming in to see their work and to ask them questions about their animals.

4. Divide students into pairs and have students give mini-demonstrations to each other, sharing the things on display. Allow time for them to ask each other questions. Once this has been completed, allow small groups to go around the room in your classroom to see the work of other students in class. Rotate the groups so that all students have a chance to walk around the room, and a chance to give their presentations.

Optional Ideas

Enlist the help of your students to decorate your classroom in the theme of animals. Play music in the background that has animal noises in it. Display posters, books, and other resources of different types of animals. You may also choose to display different stuffed animals to help decorate and add to the animal atmosphere. Brainstorm with your students for other ideas.

Assessment

Check off the appropriate publishing skill (1C) on the Teacher Checklist on page 23 of the Assessment Section. Assess student work using the Publishing Assessment Rubric on page 97.

Standards and Benchmarks: 1C, 1H

Publishing Learning Centers

The publishing phase of the writing process is the phase that involves sharing what you have learned with others. To publish is to make your work available for others to enjoy. The following learning centers will provide your students with an opportunity to share what they have learned in a variety of ways.

Silly Sentences

At this learning center, provide strips of paper for students to write some silly sentences and some true sentences about the animals they researched. Once students at the center have completed their sentences, have them share their sentences with the other students at the center. Students listen to each sentence and see if they can find the silly sentences that are not true.

Clay Critters

Provide clay at this learning center for each student to make his or her own animal. Be sure to provide the necessary materials and tools for this center to be successful. Once students have completed their critters, have them set them aside to dry. Save these clay critters for the Ask the Expert Day as outlined in Publishing Lesson 5 (see page 93.)

Animal Wheels

Have students create wheels of information about their animals. At this learning center, have the following materials ready: two paper plates, scissors, and brads. Have each student take the first paper plate and divide it into fourths. In each section of the plate, the student writes a sentence about his or her animal and a small illustration to go with it. On the second paper plate, have the student cut out one section of the paper plate to match the size of one section on the first paper plate. (You may choose to have the plates already cut and ready to go before students come to this learning center.) When students have completed their sentences and illustrations, they are to attach the top plate to the bottom plate with a brad. Only one section of the plate will be showing at a time.

Amazing Mobiles

Using six index cards and a long piece of ribbon, students can create their own mobiles. The first index card has the title of their report with an illustration. On each of the following index cards, students write a sentence from their reports about their animals, and then they illustrate each card. Starting at the top of the ribbon, students glue or paste the cards in order. Hang the mobiles to decorate your classroom.

Animal Habitats

Have a shoe box available for each student at this learning center. Using scissors, construction paper, glue, etc., students will make a model of the habitat that their animal would live in. Students may cut pictures from magazines and other resources or make their own pictures. Teach techniques for making objects look 3-D by putting some things in the center of the shoe box or coming from the top or sides. Allow students to use their imaginations as they create these "homes" for their animals.

Standards and Benchmarks: 1C, 1H

Home-School Activities

Here are some *optional* publishing activities that you can do at home with your child. These activities will enrich objectives and lessons being taught in school.

✓ Review of the Report

Your child will be bringing home the finished product of his or her research report. Sit down with your child and read the report from start to finish. Look at the illustrations accompanying the report. Ask your child questions about the animal he or she studied and the report writing process. Take a few minutes to write a note to your child in praise of his or her writing efforts. Sharing these compliments in writing will make a more permanent memory and reading your writing will also reinforce the importance and the need for writing.

✓ Dazzling Decorations

Allow your child the freedom to decorate his or her room for at least a week with items and information about the animal that he or she studied. Your child can draw pictures of his or her animal in action, and he or she can write sentences of information about the animal.

✓ Wall of Fame

Create an area in your home where your child can display good school work and other papers with information about his or her animal. Post projects and activities your child has made at school in this area. Keep an eye out for newspaper articles in your local newspaper that are about the animal your child is studying.

✓ Noteworthy News

Help your child create a newspaper all about his or her animal. This can be done on the computer or it can be done by hand. Enlist suggestions from your child about format and content. Copies of this newspaper can be made for friends and family members.

✓ Audio/Visual

If you have access to a camcorder or a cassette tape player, make a recording of your child giving a report on his or her animal. The report can list information as well as lingering questions and fun things your child learned while doing this report. Pop popcorn or make other treats the night you play the recording for your family and friends. What a fun way to celebrate learning!

✓ Field Trips from Home

If possible, plan a trip to a local zoo or other facility that may have the animal your child researched for his or her report. This can be a fun, informational outing for the entire family.

.Standards and Benchmarks: 1C, 1H

Publishing Games

Alike, but Not the Same

Have each student draw a picture of his or her animal. Divide the class into groups of four. In each group, place four pictures in the center of the table. Students divide up into pairs and each person chooses a picture. Each pair of students has a specified amount of time to write down the things that are similar and different about the animals they have chosen. When time is up, the judges check each list and award points for the similarities and differences. The team with the most points wins.

Matching Game

Give each student an index card upon which to write a fact about his or her animal without naming the animal. Tape each of these facts to the chalkboard. Next, give each student another index card. On this card each student writes the name of the animal he or she studied. Place these cards facedown in a pile. Divide the class into two teams. A person from Team A comes up and draws an animal from the index card pile. They then have 30 seconds to find the fact taped to the chalkboard that goes with that animal. If he or she gets it right, Team A gets a point. Team B goes next by drawing an animal card and matching it to a card on the chalkboard. Continue playing until everyone has had a turn. The team with the most points at the end of the game wins.

Dice Game

Each group of four or five students will need a die and a pen. Each student in the group will need a piece of paper. The object of the game is to be the first student to write ten (or more) things about the animal studied. The students take turns rolling the die. Any time the die lands on a one, the student who rolled the one begins writing words about his or her animal as quickly as he or she can. The remaining students in the group keep taking turns rolling the die. If another student rolls a one, he or she takes the pen from the first student and begins writing words about his or her animal. Play continues this way with students taking the pen from each other as they roll a one. The first player to get ten (or more) words about the research animal on his or her paper is the winner.

Twenty Questions in the Hot Seat

Divide the class into smaller groups. Each person from the group takes a turn being in the "hot seat." Group members ask this student *yes* and *no* questions about the animal that this student is researching (or another animal of this student's choice if group members already know the animal). The student in the "hot seat" answers questions with a yes or no answer. The first student to guess the animal is given a point. Play continues in this fashion until all members of the group have had a turn to be in the "hot seat."

Create an Animal

Have students work in small groups to create a new animal. What would this animal do? What would this animal eat? Where would this animal live? Have students share their new creations with the class.

Publishing Assessment Rubric

Use the rubric below to assess student progress using publishing skills. The numbers and letters in parenthesis correspond with the Teacher Checklist in the Assessment Section on pages 23 and 24.

Competent

The student can independently use strategies to edit and publish written work. (1C)

The student can independently incorporate illustrations or photos.

The student can independently write a finished product.

The student can independently share a finished product.

The student can independently write in response to literature. (1G)

The student can independently write in a variety of formats. (1H) (e.g., picture books, letters, stories, poems, and information pieces)

Emergent

The student can usually use strategies to edit and publish written work. (1C)

The student can usually incorporate illustrations or photos.

The student can usually write a finished product.

The student can usually share a finished product.

The student can usually write in response to literature. (1G)

The student can usually write in a variety of formats. (1H) (e.g., picture books, letters, stories, poems, and information pieces)

Beginner

The student requires assistance to use strategies to edit and publish written work. (1C)

The student requires assistance to incorporate illustrations or photos.

The student requires assistance to write a finished product.

The student requires assistance to share a finished product.

The student requires assistance to write in response to literature. (1G)

The student requires assistance to write in a variety of formats. (1H) (e.g., picture books, letters, stories, poems, and information pieces)

Mechanics
and
Grammar

This section of the unit is an optional section that you may pull from, as needed, while teaching the writing process. You may find that your students need assistance in writing complete sentences, or using nouns, verbs, adjectives, and adverbs in their writing. You may teach these lessons to the whole class or you may teach small groups needing more individual instruction. Feel free to pick and choose from the lessons and activities in this section.

98

Parts of Speech & Punctuation

The following terms and words are used in this section of the report writing unit. Use the guide below to assist students in learning and understanding the meaning of these words. These definitions fit the standards and objectives expected at the primary grade levels.

Declarative Sentences

Declarative sentences make a statement. These are also called "telling sentences."

Example: *The boy is riding a bike.*

Interrogative Sentences

Interrogative sentences ask a question. These are also called "asking sentences" or questions.

Example: *Are you going to the store?*

Nouns

A noun is a person, place, or thing.

Examples: (person) *Sally* likes monkeys.

(place) *California* is where I live.

(thing) Where is my *umbrella*?

Verbs

A verb is the action part of the sentence.

Example: The dog *barked*.

Adjectives

An adjective describes a noun. An adjective is a describing word.

Example: The *green* truck came.

Adverbs

An adverb describes the verb.

Example: The girl ran *quickly*.

Period

A period is used at the end of a declarative or "telling" sentence.

Example: The elephant woke up.

Question Mark

A question mark is used at the end of an interrogative sentence or a question.

Example: Where are we going?

Comma

A comma is used in a series of words.

Example: I will bring the milk, cookies, and bread.

Standards and Benchmarks: 3A, 3B

Mechanics and Grammar Lesson 1

Objective

The student will be able to use complete sentences in written compositions.

Materials

- copy of page 101, Complete Sentences, for each student
- large picture of two animals (Select two animals that are of high interest and animals about which the students are knowledgeable.)
- picture of a baby at about nine months to a year old
- colored chalk

Procedure

1. Hold up a picture of an animal. Ask students to tell you what they know about this animal. Have them share one sentence at a time. As they share a sentence, write it on the chalkboard. Do this until you have plenty of sentences to analyze. Next, using a different colored piece of chalk, separate the noun or the naming word from the verb in each sentence with a line. Show students that complete sentences have two different parts. Explain how important both parts of the sentence are to understanding what we say to each other.

2. Using a few of the sentences that students volunteered, erase the noun out of the sentence, and read it. Ask students if the sentence makes sense. Next, erase the verb, and read the sentences. Once again, ask students if it is a clear thought. Will others who read the sentence know what it means?

3. Next, hold up the picture of a baby. Explain to them that as a baby, they just used one word at a time. But as they grew, they learned more and more words, and now they know how to speak in complete sentences. Have each student turn to a buddy sitting next to him or her and say something that a baby might say, and then say the same thing using a complete sentence. Explain to students that in our writing, we need to use complete sentences as well so that the person reading our writing will know what we are trying to say.

4. Distribute the copies of Complete Sentences. Have students complete the page. When they have finished, go over the answers together as a class. Circulate around the room to spot any children who may be having a difficult time with this concept.

Portfolio Piece

Hold up the other picture of an animal and have students write three complete sentences about this animal. When completed, have students date their work and place it in their portfolios.

Assessment

- Check to see that students have completed the page, Complete Sentences, correctly.
- Check off the appropriate mechanics and grammar skills (3A, 3B) on the Teacher Checklist on page 24 of the Assessment Section. Assess student work by using the Mechanics and Grammar Assessment Rubric on page 122.

Complete Sentences

What is a sentence? A sentence is a complete thought with a noun, a verb, and a punctuation mark at the end. Draw lines to match the groups of words to make sentences. Then write the sentences.

1. The fly	stalks.
2. The butterfly	creeps.
3. The snake	roars.
4. The mountain lion	slithers.
5. The snail	buzzes.
6. The leopard	peeps.
7. The chick	flutters.

1. _____

2. _____

3. _____

4. _____

5. _____

6. _____

7. _____

Standards and Benchmarks: 3A, 3C, 3I, 3J

Mechanics and Grammar Lesson 2

Objective

The student will be able to use declarative sentences in written compositions.

Materials

- student journals (see page 21)
- copies of page 103, Declarative Sentences, for students

Procedure

1. Write the following journal prompt on the chalkboard: *An animal sometimes . . . .* Have students take out their journals and finish this sentence. When students have finished, ask them to share their responses. Add their endings to the sentence next to the journal prompt on the chalkboard. Be sure to place a period at the end of each sentence.

2. Now, write the words, *Declarative Sentence*, on the chalkboard. Explain to students that they have just written a declarative sentence. Explain that a declarative sentence is a sentence that tells something about a person, place, or thing. This type of sentence always ends in a period.

3. Distribute copies of the Declarative Sentences work sheet to the students. Have them write the declarative sentences correctly.

Portfolio Piece

Have students write three declarative sentences about an animal they once saw at the zoo. Allow time for students to share their sentences in small groups. Have the group members listen to make sure that the sentences are all declarative sentences. Date the work and put it in the students' portfolios.

Assessment

- Check to see that students have completed the page, Declarative Sentences, correctly.
- Check off the appropriate mechanics and grammar skills (3A, 3C, 3I, 3J) on the Teacher Checklist on pages 24 of the Assessment Section. Assess student work by using the Mechanics and Grammar Assessment Rubric on page 122.

Declarative Sentences

Write these declarative sentences correctly.

1. the sky is blue

   _____

2. the ants follow each other in a line

   _____

3. the grasshopper jumped high

   _____

4. the moose was stuck in the river

   _____

5. the peacock is very noisy

   _____

6. the koala bear eats leaves

   _____

7. studying animals is fun

   _____

Standards and Benchmarks: 3A, 3C

Mechanics and Grammar Lesson 3

Objective

The student will be able to use interrogative sentences in written compositions.

Materials

- copy of page 105, Interrogative Sentences, for each student

Procedure

1. Tell students that you would like to play a game. Tell them you are thinking of something in the classroom, and they need to guess what it is by asking you questions. Select an object and have students begin asking questions. (Be sure to select an object that is not too easy to guess. You are trying to get as many questions as you can from your students.) As they ask you a question, write their question on the chalkboard and then answer the question. Continue in this manner until a student guesses the correct answer.

2. Upon completion of the game, direct students to look at all the questions it took to guess this object. Ask students to look at each sentence. Ask them what they notice about the sentences. Some of the answers might include the following: They are all questions, they all end in a question mark, they all begin with words such as *does, is, when, why, where, has, what, how, can,* etc. Explain to students that all of the sentences on the board are questions and that question sentences are called interrogative sentences. An *interrogative sentence* asks a question, and it always ends in a question mark.

3. Distribute copies of the Interrogative Sentences work sheet to the students. Circulate around the room to help students complete the page. Go over the answers together as a class. Have students correct their own work by adding question marks and capital letters.

Portfolio Piece

Pick another object in the classroom. Tell students you would like them to guess what it is. Have them write down on a piece of paper at least five interrogative sentences to find out what it is. When students have completed their questions, read them aloud and answer them one at a time. Check to see that all sentences end in question marks. See if students can guess the object. Have students place these samples of interrogative sentences in their portfolios.

Assessment

- Check to see that each student has completed the Interrogative Sentences work sheet correctly.

- Check off the appropriate mechanics and grammar skills (3A, 3C) on the Teacher Checklist on page 24 of the Assessment Section. Assess student work by using the Mechanics and Grammar Assessment Rubric on page 122.

Interrogative Sentences

Write each asking sentence below correctly.

1. where is the zoo

_____

2. is the dog brown or black

_____

3. how does the bird fly

_____

4. what is the cat eating

_____

5. who is making that noise

_____

Write a question about a rain cloud.

_____

_____

_____

_____

_____

Standards and Benchmarks: 3A, 3D

Mechanics and Grammar Lesson 4

Objective

The student will be able to use nouns in written compositions.

Materials

- index cards with *person*, *place*, or *thing* written on them
- copy of the Nouns work sheet (page 107) for each student
- 26 pieces of construction paper, each with a letter of the alphabet written on it
- portfolios for students
- tape

Procedure

1. Tape the index cards across the top of the chalkboard in your classroom. Ask students to come up with words that fit into these categories. Write their responses under each category. Discuss with students what a noun is. Using some of the nouns they listed on the chalkboard, make sentences to show students where the nouns are found in the sentence.

2. Divide your class into groups of five or more. Give each group four or five pieces of construction paper with the letters on them. For example, Group 1 will have five pieces of construction paper with A, B, C, D, or E, written across the top. Group 2 has the letters F, G, H, I, or J written on top of five more pieces of construction paper. Continue in this fashion with the rest of the groups and the rest of the alphabet. You may wish to shuffle the construction paper to mix up the commonly used letters with some of the more uncommon ones.

3. Have students work in groups to come up with as many nouns as they can that begin with the letters they have been assigned. Remind students that these words will be a *person, place,* or *thing.*

4. When finished, have students share the nouns that they came up with for their letters. Add any nouns that class members can think of as well. Post these small "posters" around the room for students to use as references in their writing. Students may add to these posters as they think of more nouns.

5. Distribute the copies of the Nouns work sheet and have students complete the page. Circulate around the room to see if students complete the page correctly or to see if students need assistance.

Portfolio Piece

Have students find a piece of writing in their portfolios and circle all of the nouns in it.

Assessment

- Check to see that students have completed the Nouns work sheet correctly.
- Check off the appropriate mechanics and grammar skills (3A, 3D) on the Teacher Checklist on page 24 of the Assessment Section. Assess student work by using the Mechanics and Grammar Assessment Rubric on page 122.

Nouns

Write the *noun* or the naming word in each sentence.

1. A fish can swim fast. _____

2. A tiny bird eats a lot. _____

3. A giraffe is very tall. _____

4. A newborn kitten is cute. _____

5. The spotted dog is barking. _____

6. The mouse eats quickly. _____

7. The silly monkey is swinging. _____

Write three sentences below and underline the naming part or the noun.

_____

_____

_____

_____

_____

Standards and Benchmarks: 3A, 3E

Mechanics and Grammar Lesson 5

Objective

The student will be able to use verbs in written compositions.

Materials

- copy of page 109, Verbs, for each student
- piece of blank white paper for each student
- crayons or colored pencils for students
- old magazines to cut up
- scissors
- glue
- large piece of butcher paper with *Vivid Verbs* written on it
- students portfolios

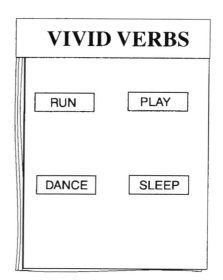

Procedure

1. Begin by asking all the things that students can do with their hands, feet, neck, legs, arms, etc. What are some of the actions that your body can do? (Some possible answers could include: jump, skip, swing, hop, etc.) List each of these words on the chalkboard. Explain to students that these are action words. Another name for these words is verbs. A *verb* is the action part of the sentence. The verb describes what the noun is doing.

2. Give each student a piece of paper. Show students how to fold the paper into fourths. In each section, students will be writing a verb. Let students select the verbs from the list on the chalkboard or let them come up with their own as long as they are approved by you. Have students illustrate the verbs with a picture that shows the action word.

3. Have students share their verb drawings in a small group. Next, distribute old magazines for students to cut out pictures that show action. Take each of these cutout pictures and post them on the large poster entitled *Vivid Verbs*. Students may use this poster as a reference in their writing. As an extension, and as a review, have students create sentences using the nouns on the alphabet poster (See Noun Lesson on page 106) and the verbs from the poster made in this lesson.

4. Distribute copies of the Verbs work sheet and have students complete this page.

Portfolio Piece

Have students pull out a piece of writing from their portfolios and underline all the verbs they can find.

Assessment

- Check to see that students have completed the Verbs work sheet correctly.
- Check off the appropriate mechanics and grammar skills (3A, 3E) on the Teacher Checklist on page 24 of the Assessment Section. Assess student work by using the Mechanics and Grammar Assessment Rubric on page 122.

Verbs

Pick the correct action word from the word box to finish each sentence. When the sentence is filled in, you will know a new fact about each animal.

live	hatch	swings	eats
stands	lays	runs	gathers

1. The monkey _____ in the trees.

2. The cheetah _____ very fast.

3. The baby giraffe _____ six feet tall.

4. Parrot chicks _____ after 28 days.

5. The ostrich _____ the largest egg.

6. The penguin _____ krill.

7. The mouse _____ food.

8. Zebras _____ in large groups.

Standards and Benchmarks: 3A, 3F

Mechanics and Grammar Lesson 6

Objective
The student will be able to use adjectives in written compositions.

Materials
- copy of page 111, Adjectives, for each student
- stuffed animal
- 9" x 12" (23 cm x 30 cm) construction paper for each student
- old magazines or newspapers to cut up
- scissors and glue
- copy of page 112, Venn Diagram, for each student

Procedure
1. Prominently display the stuffed animal that you have brought to class. Ask students to use words to describe the animal. They may also use words to describe the live animal. Record all of their responses on the chalkboard. Tell students that the words they shared are adjectives, words used to describe nouns.

2. Next, give each student a piece of construction paper, scissors, glue, and old magazines or newspapers to cut up. Have them select a noun (person, place, or thing) that they would like to describe. Students cut out a picture and paste it to the center of the page. Then have students draw five lines extending from the picture. Students will then write five adjectives to describe the picture. On the back, have the students write a sentence using each of the adjectives. Provide time for students to share their work with the other students.

3. Distribute copies of the Adjectives work sheet and have students complete it. Go over the answers together as a class. Provide assistance to those students who may need additional help.

Portfolio Piece
Distribute the Venn Diagram to the students. Students will use adjectives to describe two nouns. (Types of food work well for this activity.) Inside one of the circles, have students write one noun. Inside the other circle, have students write the other noun. In the center part where the two circles overlap, write the word *both*. Students write adjectives in each section of the Venn diagram. Where the circles intersect, students write adjectives that describe both of the nouns.

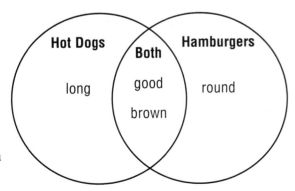

Assessment
- Check to see that students have completed the Adjectives work sheet and the Venn Diagram correctly.
- Check off the appropriate mechanics and grammar skills (3A, 3F) on the Teacher Checklist on page 24 of the Assessment Section. Assess student work by using the Mechanics and Grammar Rubric Assessment on page 122.

Adjectives

An adjective is a describing word. An adjective tells what kind and how many. An adjective describes a noun.

what kind:	The bear is *brown*.
what kind:	The *large* elephant tripped.
how many:	The chick is *four* days old.
how many:	There are *eight* boys in my class.

Write the adjective from the box that best fits each sentence.

> green   sharp   huge   eight   gray

1. The rock is _____.

2. The _____ elephant swung his trunk.

3. The parrot's feathers are _____.

4. The bear is a_____ animal.

5. An ostrich is _____ feet tall.

Write adjectives to describe the following nouns:

_____ chimpanzee

_____ frog

_____ goat

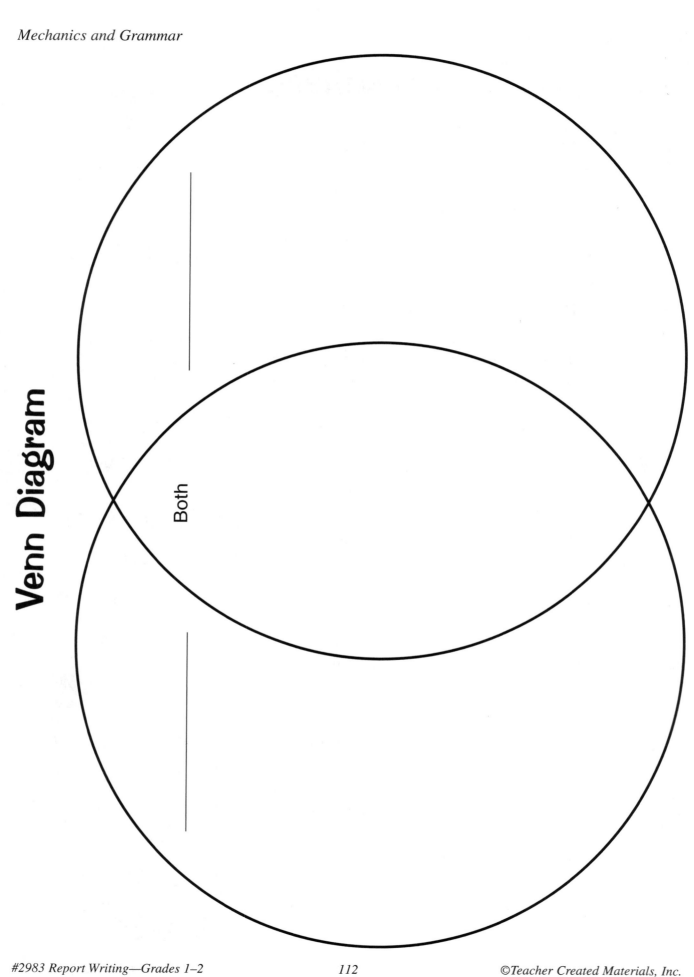

Venn Diagram

Both

Standards and Benchmarks: 3A, 3G

Mechanics and Grammar Lesson 7

Objective

The student will be able to use adverbs in written compositions.

Materials

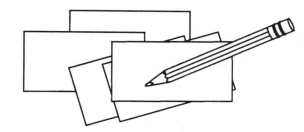

- copy of page 114, Adverbs, for each student
- index cards for each student
- bowls

Procedure

1. Hand out the Adverbs work sheet. Go through examples of what an adverb is. Write some sentences on the board as examples and underline the adverbs. Have students volunteer other adverbs. Write their responses on the chalkboard. Work with students to complete the Adverbs work sheet. Check the answers together, as a class.

2. Divide your class into two teams. Distribute an index card to each student. Have one team write a verb on each of their index cards. The other team writes an adverb on each of their cards. You may need to give more assistance to the adverb team. (Students may use adverbs that were previously listed on the chalkboard.) Examples of verbs might be *run, skip, sleep, fly,* etc. Examples of adverbs might be *happily, slowly, angrily, brightly, quickly,* etc.

3. Next put all the names of Team A in a bowl, and all the names of Team B in another bowl. Pull out a student's name from each bowl. These two students form a pair. Using the verb and the adverb listed on their cards, they are to act out the verb and the adverb together. See if the rest of the class can guess what the verb and the adverb are.

Portfolio Piece

Have students write letters to their parents telling them what they did today. Students are to use at least three adverbs (or more for some students) in their letters. Allow time for students to share their letters aloud with partners. Store these in the students' portfolios.

Assessment

- Check to see that students have completed the Adverbs work sheet correctly.
- Read through the student letters and check for the three adverbs.
- Check off the appropriate mechanics and grammar skills (3A, 3G) on the Teacher Checklist on page 24 of the Assessment Section. Assess student work by using the Mechanics and Grammar Assessment Rubric on page 122.

Adverbs

An adverb is a describing word. An adverb describes a verb.

- They ran **quickly**.
- The bear growled **loudly**.

- A cat **quietly** walked.
- The dog worked **hard** to get free.

Write the adverb that describes the underlined verb in each sentence.

1. The bird quickly <u>flew</u> away. _____

2. I carefully <u>rubbed</u> the horse. _____

3. The bears slowly <u>crept</u> into the cave. _____

4. The rabbit quietly <u>hopped</u> away. _____

5. The lion <u>roared</u> loudly. _____

6. The sparrows <u>chirped</u> happily. _____

7. A polar bear <u>swam</u> slowly. _____

8. The monkey <u>dropped</u> hurriedly. _____

9. A penguin hungrily <u>gobbled</u> food. _____

10. The wind <u>blew</u> gently. _____

   ©*Teacher Created Materials, Inc.*

Standards and Benchmarks: 3A, 3I

Mechanics and Grammar Lesson 8

Objective
The student will be able to use capital letters in first and last names and the first word in each sentence.

Materials
- copy of page 116, Capitalization, for each student
- newspapers
- scissors, glue, highlighter markers, tape
- large piece of butcher paper with the words, *First Name, Last Name, First Word in Sentence,* and *Other* written on it

Procedure
1. Begin this lesson by putting your class into groups of three or four. Distribute newspapers, markers, and scissors to each group. Tell students that you will be sending them on a scavenger hunt. Explain that they will be looking for capital letters. Ask students if they know what a capital letter is. Ask for volunteers to share examples of when to use a capital letter. (The standard for this level is that students will be able to use capital letters in first and last names and the first word of each sentence. However, some students may be aware of other times when capital letters are needed. Allow students to share these examples as well.)

2. Next, instruct the students to search throughout their newspapers for examples of capital letters. When they find a capital letter, have them highlight it. After they have highlighted a page, have them cut out the words with the capital letters. Students will then bring their words up to the butcher paper and tape them into the right category. After most students have had a chance to add words to your chart, have a discussion with students on the importance of using capitalization in their writing. Look over the examples and have students make observations about the capital letters they found.

3. Distribute the copies of the Capitalization work sheet to the students. This will give them more practice in using capital letters.

Portfolio Piece
Using the letter that students wrote to their parents (see Adverb lesson on page 113), have students circle all of the capital letters in it. If they see a letter that needs to be capitalized, have them correct it.

Assessment
- Check to see that students have completed the Capitalization work sheet correctly.
- Check off the appropriate mechanics and grammar skills (3A, 3I) on the Teacher Checklist on page 24 of the Assessment Section. Assess student work by using the Mechanics and Grammar Rubric Assessment on page 122.

Capitalization

Capital letters are used at the beginning of a sentence and for all proper nouns.

My family is going to **N**ew **Y**ork.
We went to see **U**ncle **F**red.
Doctor **J**ones said that my dog is sick.
We got a new kitten for **C**hristmas.

Write the sentences correctly. They are missing the capital letters.

1. we went to the San diego Zoo.

_____

2. february 2 is groundhog Day.

_____

3. kathey and i saw a rattlesnake.

_____

4. i hope that the pet shop has hamsters.

_____

5. aunt sally is coming to see us Friday.

_____

Write a sentence that has two capital letters in it.

_____

_____

Standards and Benchmarks: 3A, 3J

Mechanics and Grammar Lesson 9

Objective

The student will be able to use periods, question marks, and commas in sentences.

Materials

- 9" x 12" (23 cm x 30 cm) pieces of construction paper
- copy of page 118, Punctuation, for each student

Preparation

Write a period, a question mark, and a comma each on a piece of construction paper. Tape them each to a chair. Arrange the three chairs in a row at the front of the classroom.

Procedure

1. Begin the lesson by telling students you will be discussing punctuation marks today. Review when to use the period, the question mark, and the comma in a series. Write examples of these being used in sentences on the chalkboard. Discuss with students how the voice changes when these punctuation marks are being used. Demonstrate a few examples of this, and then read some sentences together, as a class, changing the voice. Distribute copies of the Punctuation work sheet for students to do. Check this page together as a class. Have students make corrections as needed.

2. For this next activity, divide the class into two teams. On the chalkboard, write a sentence that is missing one punctuation mark. The first team has a student read the sentence and see what punctuation mark is missing from the sentence. The student then goes to sit in the chair with the correct punctuation mark. If the student is right, his or her team is awarded a point. Then the second team sends a student and another sentence is written on the board. Play continues in this manner until all students have had a turn to go. The team with the most points earned is the winner.

Portfolio Piece

Using a piece of writing from their portfolio, have students read aloud and use their voice and inflection to show the punctuation marks being used.

Assessment

- Check to see that students have completed the Punctuation work sheet correctly.
- Check off the appropriate mechanics and grammar skills (3A, 3J) on the Teacher Checklist on page 24 of the Assessment Section. Assess student work by using the Mechanics and Grammar Assessment Rubric on page 122.

Punctuation

Periods and question marks are punctuation marks. They come at the end of sentences.

I want to go to the Desert Museum. Do you want to go too?

Write the sentences below. Use the correct end mark for each sentence.

1. Do iguanas eat fruit

_____

2. I like to see the swans fly

_____

3. Is the crane a bird

_____

4. The bear began to run

_____

A comma is a punctuation mark that comes inside the sentence.

I saw an eagle, a crane, and a hawk the other day.

Write the sentences below correctly. Put commas in the right places.

5. It is a book about wolves bears and foxes.

_____

_____

6. I saw a planet a falling star and the moon.

_____

_____

7. Is Sea World in California Florida or Texas?

_____

_____

Standards and Benchmarks: 3A, 3B, 3C, 3D, 3E, 3F, 3G, 3H, 3I, 3J

Mechanics and Grammar Learning Centers

Silly Sentences

Have students write sentences on strips of paper. Cut the sentences in half separating the noun and the verb. Have students piece the halves together at random to come up with silly sentences. Have them write all the sentences on a piece of paper. See who can find the silliest sentence.

Is It a Sentence?

Ahead of time, write sentences and sentence fragments on strips of paper. When students come to this center, they are to draw a line down the center of their paper. Taking a strip of paper, students read it and determine whether or not it is a complete sentence. If it is a sentence, they write it under the sentence column. If it is not, they write it under the sentence fragment column. Have an answer key handy for students to check their own work.

Spelling Practice

Have students make a list of words that they want to use in their reports or other writing. Have them look up the spelling of each word in the dictionary and write its definition. Finally, have them list whether the word is a noun, a verb, an adjective, or an adverb.

A Picture is Worth a Thousand Words

Gather a bunch of pictures from magazines, posters, etc., and place them at the table. As students come to the center, they pick a picture and write three to six sentences about it. When they have completed this, have them read their sentences and make any needed changes. Then have them share their pictures and writing with a partner. Have students edit their writing again after hearing their partners' comments. Could any of these sentences be the beginning of a story?

A Day in the Life of a . . .

Place a stuffed animal at this learning center and provide pencils and paper. Ask students to think about what this animal would be doing if it came to spend the day with them. Describe in detail the comings and goings of a day in the life of the animal at their home. What would the animal eat, do, play, and where would it sleep? When finished, have students check punctuation, capitalization, and spelling.

Who? What? Where? When? Why?

Make a page with these questions across the top. Have students answer each question with a complete sentence using an experience they have recently had. Working with a buddy, have students share their work and edit each other's writing. When finished, have students illustrate the event. Be sure that the picture also shows the who, what, where, when, and why of what happened.

Standards and Benchmarks: 3A, 3B, 3C, 3D, 3E, 3F, 3G, 3H, 3I, 3J

Home-School Activities

Here are some *optional* mechanics and grammar activities that can be done at home. These activities will enrich objectives and lessons being taught in school.

✓ Part of Speech Day

Pick a different part of speech to focus on for a day. (We are studying the noun, verb, adjective, and adverb.) Any time that specific part of speech is heard, seen, or written, call attention to it. Point out parts of speech on signs as you drive in the car, in books you read to your child, and in your language. See how many parts of speech you can find.

✓ King or Queen for a Day

Make a crown out of yellow construction paper and decorate it with paper jewels. Use old newspapers and magazines to cut out parts of speech, and then glue them onto the crown. Your child will proudly display the words he or she is learning.

✓ Computer Craze

If you have a computer in your home, allow time for your child to type sentences. This will give him or her practice on how to make complete sentences as well as how to make punctuation marks such as periods, question marks, and commas. Letters to a friend, an imaginary story, or a daily report are all good suggestions. You may even have your child type the menu for your evening meal or a list of things you need to get done the next day.

✓ Hide and Seek

To practice using questions or interrogative sentences, take a small object and hide it somewhere in a designated room. Then ask family members to come into that room. They will try to find the object by asking you questions. You can only answer *yes* or *no* questions. When it is found, give another person a chance to hide the object.

✓ Musical Notes

Play a variety of music for your family. Have family members write down all the words they can think of to describe how the music sounds (adjectives) and how the song makes them feel like moving or acting (adverbs). Discuss, as a family, what you put on your list. Then move on to the next musical selection. Use this opportunity to talk about how the music we listen to affects us and our family members.

✓ The Tasting Table

This activity takes courage, but is lots of fun. At a meal, blindfold your child. Place a small bit of food in his or her mouth and ask him or her to describe it. How does it feel, taste, and smell? See if your child can guess the food. Next, you take a turn and see if you can describe the bit of food in your mouth! Have fun!

Standards and Benchmarks: 3A, 3B, 3C, 3D, 3E, 3F, 3G, 3H, 3I, 3J

Mechanics and Grammar Games

Twist and Turn

Using a permanent marker, draw circles on an old shower curtain. Inside each circle write one of the following words: *noun, verb, adjective,* or *adverb*. Repeat until the shower curtain is covered with circles, remembering to use only one word per circle. When the curtain is completely filled in, make the game cards. On one stack of index cards write body parts—*right arm, right leg, left arm, knee,* etc. On a second stack of cards write examples of the parts of speech written in the circles. Make sure you have an equal number of cards with adverbs (quickly, happily, etc.), adjectives (soft, brown, etc.), nouns (man, tree, etc.) and verbs (sleep, sing, etc.) on them.

To play the game, place the curtain on the floor. Have some children stand around the curtain and choose two other students to draw the cards. One student will call out a body part and one will call out a noun, verb, adverb, or adjective from the other pile of cards. The students standing around the curtain will take turns trying to put the correct body part on the right part of speech. The first person to fall steps out of the game. Play continues until only one student is left playing. Students can rotate being the callers.

Bag It!

Divide the class into small groups of three or four people. Place an item (paper clip, pencil, eraser, etc.) from your classroom into a bag for each group. Distribute the bags so that each group has one. Group members look inside the bag to see what it is without letting any other groups know. Groups then work together to write five sentences that would describe the item without giving away what it is. When all groups have prepared their sentences, they take turns presenting them to the class. Students listen as the describing sentences are read and they raise their hands to guess. The first person to guess the correct item earns a point for his or her group. The group with the most points at the end is the winner.

Go Fish

Create your own Go Fish game using a set of 48 index cards. Divide the index cards into two piles. On the first half, write *noun, verb, adverb,* or *adjective*. On the other 24 cards, write examples of each of these parts of speech. Students are dealt cards and try to find matches. A match might look like this: *noun-doll, verb-jumps, adjective-green,* or *adverb-quickly.* The student with the most matches is the winner.

Eyewitness Account

Dress up a student with a lot of clothing. Some ideas might include gloves, different colored shoes, a hat, items to carry, and more—the more items, the better. At a set time, have your students get a piece of paper and a pencil ready. Tell them you would like them to jot down words describing a special guest. Invite your dressed-up student to come into the classroom. As this student wanders around the room, students write down as many words they can think of that describe the student. Words will probably include both nouns and adjectives. Don't let the student stay in the classroom too long, but long enough for all students to get a good look. Ask the dressed-up student to leave the room. Have students compare lists. Who came up with the most nouns and adjectives? After discussing the student lists, invite the dressed-up student back into the classroom. Did students miss any items or describing words they could have used? Did any students write down items that were not on the dressed-up student?

Mechanics and Grammar Assessment Rubric

Use the rubric below to assess student progress using mechanics and grammar skills. The numbers and letters in parenthesis correspond with the Teacher Checklist (page 24) in the Assessment Section.

Competent

The student can independently use grammatical and mechanical conventions in writing. (3)

The student can independently form letters in print and space words and sentences. (3A)

The student can independently use complete sentences in written compositions. (3B)

The student can independently use declarative and interrogative sentences in writing. (3C)

The student can independently use nouns in written compositions. (3D)

The student can independently use verbs in written compositions. (3E)

The student can independently use adjectives in written compositions. (3F)

The student can independently use adverbs in written compositions. (3G)

The student can independently use conventions of spelling in written compositions. (3H)

The student can independently use conventions of capitalization in written compositions. (3I)

The student can independently use conventions of punctuation in written compositions. (3J)

Emergent

The student can usually use grammatical and mechanical conventions in writing. (3)

The student can usually form letters in print and space words and sentences. (3A)

The student can usually use complete sentences in written compositions. (3B)

The student can usually use declarative and interrogative sentences in writing. (3C)

The student can usually use nouns in written compositions. (3D)

The student can usually use verbs in written compositions. (3E)

The student can usually use adjectives in written compositions. (3F)

The student can usually use adverbs in written compositions. (3G)

The student can usually use conventions of spelling in written compositions. (3H)

The student can usually use conventions of capitalization in written compositions. (3I)

The student can usually use conventions of punctuation in written compositions. (3J)

Beginner

The student requires assistance to use grammatical and mechanical conventions in writing. (3)

The student requires assistance to form letters in print and space words and sentences. (3A)

The student requires assistance to use complete sentences in written compositions. (3B)

The student requires assistance to use declarative and interrogative sentences in writing. (3C)

The student requires assistance to use nouns in written compositions. (3D)

The student requires assistance to use verbs in written compositions. (3E)

The student requires assistance to use adjectives in written compositions. (3F)

The student requires assistance to use adverbs in written compositions. (3G)

The student requires assistance to use conventions of spelling in written compositions. (3H)

The student requires assistance to use conventions of capitalization in written compositions. (3I)

The student requires assistance to use conventions of punctuation in written compositions. (3J)

The Inquiry Journal

At this point in the unit students have, with step-by-step instruction, completed the writing process for a report. This section will give students a chance to practice some of those skills independently. Use the Inquiry Journal to do just that. The Inquiry Journal is a booklet put together with prompts on each page that will take the students through another report. Students may still need help, but the Inquiry Journal will help keep them working and moving, and it will keep all of their work in one spot.

The Inquiry Journal Overview

Teacher Note: The next few pages have an inquiry journal for students to use as they write a research report. This is to be used after students have received teaching and instruction on the research process. The Inquiry Journal is meant to be used independently by the students only after they have finished the previous sections of this report writing unit. The Inquiry Journal will prompt students on the steps of the report writing process and keep all of their research materials in one place.

Before following these page-by-page usage directions, make as many copies as needed (one book per child) of The Inquiry Journal following the assembly instructions on page 125.

Page 1: Interest Survey

Students answer the questions on this page to find a topic of interest for them to research. Discussing their surveys with another student may also help pull more ideas up.

Page 2: Brainstorming Web

Students use the web on this page to get ideas down about what they can write about the topic they have chosen. The research topic goes in the center of the web, and ideas and words related to the topic go in the outside parts of the web. Students may also draw pictures to help get their ideas down on paper.

Pages 3 and 4: Research and Note Taking

Students use this space to jot down notes they gather from books and other resources. There is plenty of room for notes, as well as a space on page 4 of the Inquiry Journal for students to write down the book title, author, and the copyright date for their bibliographies.

Page 5: Writing the Draft

Students begin writing the rough drafts of their research reports on this page. Set up the guidelines and criteria with students about how long you want their reports to be. Remind them to put a title at the top of their draft.

Page 6: Editing and Revising

This page has a proofreading chart students may use to edit their report. Have students edit their own drafts first, and then pair them with a buddy to get more editing and input. Allow students time to revise and rewrite as needed. Have students share their reports with you as the teacher. When corrections and adjustments are made, instruct students to move on to the publishing portion of the report writing process.

Publishing the Report

Students are now ready to publish their reports. Students may word process their reports on a computer. Review with students how to use spell check, the shift key, the space bar, etc. Have students print the published version of their reports. Then have students create a cover for their reports.

Standards and Benchmarks: 1A, 1B, 1C, 1D, 1E, 1F, 1H, 2A, 3A-3J

The Inquiry Journal
(Assembly Instructions)

Materials

- one piece of 9" x 12" (23 cm x 30 cm) construction paper per student
- copy of pages 125–128 for each student
- scissors
- stapler
- felt tip marker

Instructions for Making an Inquiry Journal

1. Cut the construction paper in half so that you have two 6" x 9" (15 cm x 23 cm) pieces. Lay one piece on a flat surface.

2. Cut out the journal pages and stack them pages 1 (top) to 6 (bottom). Place stacked pages directly on top of the construction paper. Make certain the book pages' left edges are flush with the construction paper's left edge.

3. Place the second half of construction paper on top of page 1. Line up the left edges of all sheets. Staple them along the edge to create a spine.

4. Using the felt tip marker on the construction paper cover, write My Inquiry Journal and Name (see illustration below), or cut out the bottom of this page and glue it onto the construction paper cover.

My
Inquiry Journal

Name _____

My Inquiry Journal

Interest Survey

Answer the questions to come up with a topic to research.

1. Activities I like to do are _____

2. The country I would like to visit is _____

3. The kind of games I like are _____

4. I like to read books about_____

5. I wish I could learn how to _____

6. My favorite outdoor place is _____

Check the boxes that you are interested in:

_____ dancing on stage   _____ the ocean

_____ flying a plane   _____ living in another country

_____ taking pictures   _____ computers

_____ dinosaurs   _____ make-believe stories

What would you like to write a report about?

Brainstorming Web

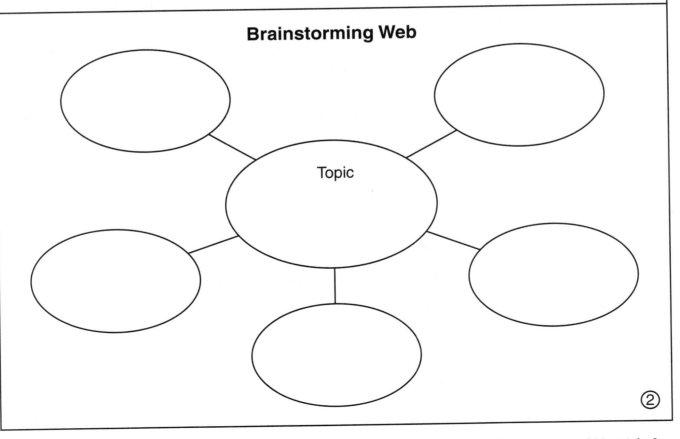

My Inquiry Journal *(cont.)*

Research and Note Taking

③

Research and Note Taking

Bibliography Notes

Book Title _____

Author _____

Copyright Date _____

④

My Inquiry Journal *(cont.)*

Writing the Draft

⑤

Editing and Revising

☐ Does my report make sense?

☐ Is my report interesting?

☐ Have I left anything out?

☐ Have I used describing words?

☐ Are there words or sentences that don't belong?

Take out something.	⌒
Add a comma.	⌒
Add a period.	⊙
Begin a new paragraph.	¶
Make a capital letter.	≡
Make a lower case letter.	/lc
Word is spelled wrong.	◯sp

⑥

The Observation Report

The observation report is another type of report that is a variation of the standard report taught to students in the classroom. The difference with this report is that the research portion is done actively, using the senses instead of books and other resources. For those students who have a difficult time reading, the observation report offers students an opportunity to apply research skills in the writing process without using books and other materials.

The observation report can also be an enjoyable new way to write a report. The same steps (brainstorming, researching, drafting, revising and editing, and publishing) are used with the observation report. The observation report also lends itself to some other subject areas, such as science.

Standards and Benchmarks: 1A, 1B, 1C, 1D, 1E, 1F, 1H, 2A, 3A–3J

The Observation Report Overview

There are many types of reports that students are asked to write. One of these is the observation report. The writing process is still used to write this report. Use the guidelines below to help students write an observation report.

Brainstorming

Topics for observation reports are generally assigned. A topic will be given to students to observe, but brainstorming will be necessary to pull up information that students already know. Using a brainstorming web (see page 28) can focus a student's ideas.

Ideas for Observation Reports

- Observation of science projects
- Observations of an athletic game
- Observations of nature and the world
- Observations of a young child or baby
- Observations of a conversation between two people

Researching

Students will be gathering their information in a variety of ways. Students may still use books and resources, but they will also need to rely on their observations to note changes and results. This type of research is more active. Students will be collecting data to use for their observation reports.

Drafting

Using the data collected from the observations, students begin drafting and writing the observation report. The outline for the observation report follows the same criteria as the research report: title, an opening sentence, three middle sentences, and an ending sentence. Students may write more or less depending on their level and skills. Students at higher levels should be writing more than one paragraph.

Editing and Revising

Once the draft has been written, students need to edit and revise their observation report. First, have students edit their own reports, looking for punctuation, grammar, or spelling mistakes. Then have students read each other's drafts to offer suggestions for improvement. Finally, if needed, a teacher's advice would be helpful in revising the observation report.

Publishing

The best format for publishing an observation report would be word processing it on the computer. Remember to help students spell check and space their reports. Have students include small illustrations depicting each stage of the observation report. On the next few pages you will find observation reports that can be done with your class.

Standards and Benchmarks: 1A, 1B, 1C, 1D, 1E, 1F, 1H, 2A, 3A–3J

Observation Report Lesson 1

Objective

The student will be able to record reactions and observations.

Materials

- hard boiled egg for each group of students
- jar with a lid for each group of students
- vinegar
- copy of page 136, The Rubber Egg, for each student

Preparation

Write a number on the bottom of each jar and assign each group a number so that they know which jar is theirs throughout the experiment.

Procedure

1. Divide your class into smaller groups. Give each group a jar and a hard-boiled egg.

2. Have students record their observations about the egg before anything is done to it on The Rubber Egg work sheet.

3. Encourage students to predict what will happen to the egg when it is placed in the vinegar.

4. Place the hard-boiled egg in the jar and pour vinegar over the top. Screw the lid on the jar. Periodically observe the egg for three days. Students will be making observations and taking notes each day to use in their observation reports. Set aside a specific time each day to observe the egg and note changes and observations.

Teacher's Information: After three days of being in the vinegar, the egg will have a rubber texture. The shell will have lost its hardness, and the egg will feel like a rubber egg.

Portfolio Piece

Have students write a letter telling someone about this experiment. Students may use their notes to help them remember their observations. Instruct students to use at least three adjectives to describe the egg, after three days, in their letter.

Assessment

- Check to see that students have completed the experiment, The Rubber Egg, correctly.
- Check off the observation report skills (1A, 1F, 3F) on the Teacher Checklist. (See pages 23 and 24 of the Assessment Section.)

Standards and Benchmarks: 1A, 1B, 1C, 1D, 1E, 1F, 1H, 2A, 3A-3J

Observation Report Lesson 2

Objective

The student will use the writing process to write an observation report.

Materials

- pencils
- notebook for each student
- copy of page 133, The Spectator Sport, for each student
- copy of page 134, Give Me Five!, for each student

Procedure

1. Students will need to observe (research) the world around them to write this observation report. Be sure to use the steps of the writing process (see page 130, The Observation Report Overview.) as students do these reports. Many observation reports can be done right in your classroom or just outside on school grounds.

2. The first observation report is done by sitting quietly and observing the world around you. Students will record what they hear, see, touch, smell, etc. Distribute copies of The Spectator Sport. Go over the directions with students. Go with students to find a spot outside to take notes and make observations.

3. Upon returning to the classroom, have students use their notes and observations to write a draft of their observation report. The Give Me Five! work sheet will help students record the main ideas. In the center of the hand, students write the title. On each finger, students write an idea for the report. Using this outline, students then write the draft of the observation report.

4. Pair students with buddies. They will read each other's drafts and offer suggestions for any editing or corrections. Have students discuss the similarities and differences of what they observed outside. After students have written their drafts, and these have been read and edited (at appropriate student level) by their partners, students will rewrite their drafts in preparation for the final draft.

Portfolio Piece

Have students illustrate a picture of what they saw while doing the observation report research. Attach this picture to the final copy of the observation report.

Technology Connection

Have students use a word-processing program to type their observation reports. Assist students in using spell check.

Assessment

Have students turn in their notes, the draft with editing marks, the final draft, and the illustration. Check to see that each stage is done correctly. Check off the appropriate skills on the Teacher Checklist on pages 23–24.

Extension

Use page 135, Observation Report Suggestions, for more ideas of observation reports that you can do with your students.

The Spectator Sport

For this observation report you need to use your senses (hearing, seeing, feeling, touching, etc.). Follow the steps below for this spectator sport observation report.

Selecting a Spot

What location should you choose? Is there a spot on the playground? How about a room in your house? or the school cafeteria? How about somewhere in your classroom? Be sure to pick a spot that has a lot of action going on.

Brainstorming

What do you already know about this place? What sounds, sights, and actions do you expect to find?

Researching

Take in as much of your surroundings as you can. Do not talk to other people so that you can concentrate on your report. Using a notebook, jot down notes of what you see, hear, smell, and feel. Write down all the people, places, or things involved. What do the surroundings look like? Write down all the noises you hear. Is it noisy or quiet? Write down how it feels. Is it cold, warm, dry, wet? What do you smell? Record as much of the sights, sounds, smells, and actions as you can.

Drafting

Review your notes and decide what you are going to write about in your observation report. Select a title and jot down the topics about which you want to write a sentence. Use page 134, Give Me Five!, to record your main ideas. Using this outline, write the draft of your observation report.

Editing and Revising

Read through your report. Read it to someone else or have someone read it so that you can hear it. What is it missing? Do you need to add anything? Correct any punctuation, grammar, and spelling errors.

Publishing

You are ready to publish your observation report. Type it into the computer. Remember to use spell check to review your spelling. Select a graphic to go with your report and you are ready to go!

Give Me Five!

In the center of the hand, write the title of your observation report. Write an idea for the report on each finger.

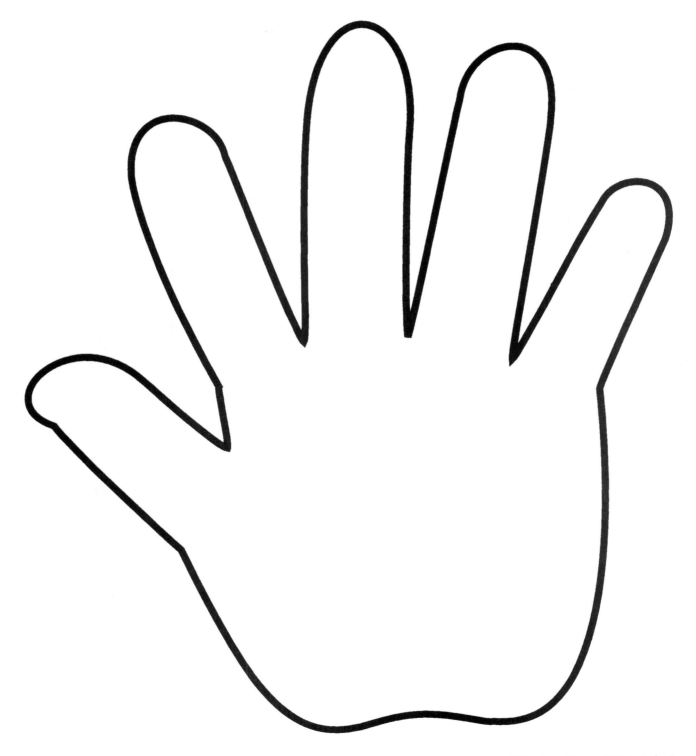

134

Standards and Benchmarks: 1A, 1B, 1C, 1D, 1E, 1F, 1H, 2A, 3A–3J

Observation Report Suggestions

There are many types of observation reports that students can write. Before leaving the classroom to go on the *observation walk,* give clear directions on what they are looking for and the notes they will be making. Spend time brainstorming as a class about what they think they will find on the walk. Be sure to allow time in the process for students to write a draft of their findings and to complete the published version. Select one or more from the following options:

Shape Observation Report

Take a walk around the school looking for natural shapes. Find two of each of the following: circle, triangle, square, rectangle, and diamond. Have students take notes in their notebooks.

Question Observation Report

Before leaving the classroom, have students brainstorm questions they would like to have answered. As they take this walk, they are recording as many questions as they can think of relating to the things around them. Upon returning to the classroom, students may select a question they would like to have answered. They can ask other people, research in books, or use other resources to find the answer.

Color Observation Report

In notebooks, students write down as many colors as they can see or choose one color and find as many things as the can in the same color. Students can also find different shades of the same colors.

Coin Flip Observation Report

To start this walk, students flip a coin to decide whether they will be going right or left (heads go left, tails go right). Students record every observation they see as they make their way back to the classroom. Students are looking at interesting objects. After they have stopped to look at objects closely, they flip the coin again to determine the next direction.

Living and Nonliving Observation Report

On this walk, have students record observations and notes about the living and nonliving things they find. Were there more living or nonliving things found on the walk?

Up, Down, and All-Around Observation Report

While students take this observation walk, have them look in a specific direction (down, for example.) Students write everything they can see looking down. Then have students take the same walk looking up, and record their observations. Take the walk again and have students look all around. Have students look at their notes. What are the differences in what they saw on the different walks?

The Rubber Egg

Day One

Look at and feel the egg before you put it in the vinegar. List six words (adjectives) that describe it.

_____ _____ _____

_____ _____ _____

What is your prediction? What do you think will happen to the egg?

_____

Day Two

What observations do you notice about your egg after it has been in the vinegar for a day?

_____

Would you like to change your prediction?

_____

Day Three

What did the egg look like after you took it out of the vinegar?

_____

How did the egg feel after you took it out of the vinegar?

_____

What happened to the shell?

_____

Write a draft of what you observed with at least five sentences. This will be your observation report. Be sure to have a title, opening sentence, three middle sentences, and a good ending sentence.

The Oral Report

This final section of the report writing unit is the oral report. Many times the research report and the oral report go hand in hand, but many times, students lack instruction and practice on how to give an oral presentation. This section of the unit has lessons that will give students practice and instruction on an oral presentation of the report they have written. Some students may even find the oral presentation easier than the report writing.

Standards and Benchmarks: 1F, 2A

Oral Report Lesson 1

Objective

The student will be able to share an oral report with a detailed description.

Materials

- 3 to 5 index cards per student
- crayons or colored pencils

Procedure

1. This is the first oral presentation the students in your classroom have probably ever given. They may have seen someone else give an oral presentation. Ask students what is involved in giving an oral presentation. Some responses may include the following: It is scary to stand in front of a lot of people, you get to use a microphone, you need to read off of a paper, etc. Tell students that some of these same things may take place when they give an oral presentation of their report. Assure them that you will help them every step of the way to make this a positive experience.

2. The first thing students need to do is put some notes together that they can use while they are giving an oral presentation. Distribute index cards to students. (Start with three index cards.) Then ask students to think of three things they learned while doing their research report that they really want to share with the class. Have them write these thoughts on their index cards. Each thought or sentence needs to be written on just one card so that the ideas don't run together. Some students may be able to complete more than three index cards, meaning they have more things to share in their report.

3. Students may use their written reports to write these index cards. Remind them to think of what they want to share first. The first item needs to be attention-getting and interesting. Next, they can share other facts and details about their report. The more specific information they give, the more interesting the report will seem to the listeners.

4. Distribute the crayons or colored pencils. On each note card, have students draw a small picture that goes with what is written on the card. This will help prompt students (especially non-readers or beginning readers) to remember what they have written.

5. On presentation day, divide your class into small groups so that it is less intimidating for students. Have students take turns sharing their oral reports. Before dividing up into groups, instruct the listeners to think of questions or supportive comments they may give the presenters when the report is finished. This will encourage students to listen and participate as the report is being given.

Assessment

Check off the oral report skills (1F, 2A) on the Teacher Checklist on pages 23 and 24 of the Assessment Section.

Standards and Benchmarks: 1A

Oral Report Lesson 2

Objective

The student will be able to discuss and share ideas with peers.

Materials

- small paper bag for each student
- crayons or colored pencils for students
- items for "sample bag"
- old magazines to cut up
- scissors

Procedure

1. Students will be sharing with the class the things they have learned from their research reports. This can be a difficult and scary thing for children. This lesson is sure to help prompt them in remembering what to say for their oral reports.

2. When students give their oral reports, they pull one item out of the bag to trigger their memories. You may put together a sample bag like the following: If you are doing an oral report on dogs, you could put some dog food (the food a dog needs to eat), a leash (dogs need exercise), a picture of a dog (what a dog looks like), a piece of paper with the word *friend* (dog is a man's best friend) written on it, and a play bone (dogs like to play). These items will be reminders of what to talk about for the oral presentation of the report.

3. Distribute the paper bags for students to put together their own oral presentation bags. Students may illustrate their own pictures or they may find pictures from old magazines. Using the crayons or colored pencils, students should also decorate the outside of the bags to add interest. Students take the bags home and fill them with at least five things that have to do with their reports. (The number of items may be altered to fit the needs of the students in your class.)

4. On presentation day, divide your class into small groups so that it is less intimidating for students. Have students take turns sharing their oral reports. Before dividing up into groups, instruct the listeners to think of questions or supportive comments they may give the presenters when the report is finished. This will encourage students to listen and participate as the report is being given.

Technology Connection

Students may need to look up pictures of their animals on the Internet. Some of the animals that students have studied may not be common enough to be found in magazines and other materials. Aid students in printing these pictures to include in their bags.

Assessment

Check off the oral report skill (1A) on the Teacher Checklist on page 23 of the Assessment Section.

Standards and Benchmarks: 1C

Oral Report Lesson 3

Objective

The student will incorporate illustrations and visual aids into their oral presentation.

Materials

- small paper bag for each student
- crayons or colored pencils for students
- yarn, felt, fake fur, ribbon, or other materials for puppets
- puppet show stage

Procedure

1. One of the most comforting things to have when giving an oral presentation is support. In this lesson, students will be making a puppet of the animal they have been researching to give the report for them.

2. Distribute the paper bags for students to color and decorate. It would be best for students to sketch their puppet face on a piece of paper before beginning to draw it on the paper bag. Using the crayons, colored pencils, and other materials available, students decorate the bags so that they look like the animal they are giving a report on.

3. Next, give students a chance to practice their oral presentations using their new puppet friends. Students may practice using their desks as the puppet show stage. Allow plenty of time for students to rehearse and get used to using their puppets.

4. On presentation day, set up a real puppet show stage to add to the authenticity. Have students take turns sharing their oral reports before the class. Before the reports begin, instruct the listeners to think of questions or supportive comments they may give the presenters when the report is finished. This will encourage students to listen and participate as the report is being given.

Portfolio Piece

Place the animal puppets in the student portfolios. Give the students the assignment of taking their puppets home to share the oral presentation with family members. Students will love the opportunity to share what they have learned in such a comfortable way.

Assessment

Check off the oral report skill (1C) on the Teacher Checklist on page 23 of the Assessment Section.

Standards and Benchmarks: 1B

Oral Report Lesson 4

Objective

The student will incorporate suggestions from peers and teachers on his or her oral presentation.

Materials

- tape cassette player or camcorder

Procedure

1. This lesson can be used along with any of the previous lessons on giving oral presentations. To begin, set aside time for each student to read or present his or her report on cassette tape or videotape (depending on what you have available.)

2. Next, divide the students up into groups of two students. Discuss, as a class, ahead of time, what it means to offer suggestions or advice to another student. Explain that each student has had the opportunity to record his or her report on cassette or videotape. Now some feedback is needed for students to make improvements. Each student will have the chance to be the presenter (on tape) and the listener. When the student is in the role of listener, he or she will look for things to say that would help make the presentation even better. Have the listener think of at least two things to offer as suggestions. (The number of suggestions may be altered depending on the level of your students.) Share examples of things that a listener may say. Some examples might include these: "You do a nice job of talking loud enough, but you are talking too fast for me to hear all of the words," or "You spoke slowly enough to follow along, and I liked the thing you said about monkeys loving bananas."

3. Students take turns being the listener and watching their own presentations. Allow time for students to give their oral presentations again, either on cassette or videotape. Using the second copy, set aside a time that these will be shown to the whole class.

4. Spend time after the presentations asking students to share what comments, advice, or suggestions helped them improve their oral presentations. Discuss the importance of getting suggestions and ideas from a different person. Explain the value in revising and making needed adjustments to better our work. It would also be a good opportunity to discuss how to give good suggestions and advice. The more specific the advice, the better, as it gives a clear understanding of what needs to be improved and how to change it.

Assessment

Check off the oral report skill (1B) on the Teacher Checklist on page 23 of the Assessment Section.

Bibliography

Caulkins, Lucy. *The Art of Teaching Writing.* Heinemann, 1994.

Graves, Donald. *Children Want to Write.* Heinemann, 1982.

Graves, Donald and Virginia Stuart. *Write from the Start.* Dutton, 1985.

McClanahan, Elaine and Carolyn Wicks. *Future Force: Kids That Want to, Can, and Do!*: *A Teacher's Handbook.* Pact Publishing, 1994.

Sebranek, Patrick, Verne Meyer, and Dave Kemper. *Write Source 2000.* Houghton Mifflin Company Publishing House, 1999.

Silberman, Arlene. *Growing up Writing: Teaching Children to Write, Think, and Learn.* Time Books, 1991.

Teacher Resources

http://www.thewritesource.com/topics.htm
Grade level appropriate writing topics and ideas for students

http://www.odyssey.on.ca/~elaine.coxon/rubrics.htm
Help for writing your own rubrics for report writing

http://www.bced.gov.bc.ca/irp/elak7/
Assessment techniques and strategies for assessing writing

http://www.ipl.org
Internet Public Library

http://www.onelook.com/index.html
Online dictionary

http://www.thesaurus.com/
Online thesaurus

http://www.users.interport.net/~hdu/referenc.htm
A Web site for finding and using information on the Internet

http://www.fwsd.wednet.edu/cur/targets/K/index.html
Examples of kindergarten writing

Answer Key

Page 41

1. dictionary
2. An encyclopedia is a book or set of books with information on a variety of subjects.
3. It is book that is factual in content.
4. Answers will vary.
5. Answers will vary.
6. Answers will vary.

Page 46

1. A table of contents lists what is in a book and on which page it can be found.
2. It is at the beginning of a book.
3. Answers will vary.
4. Answers will vary.

Page 55

Telling Sentences
The sky is blue.
He is happy.
They like school.
Greg talks a lot.

Asking Sentences
What is his name?
How much is it?
Where is the book?
How old are they?

Page 60

(Answers will vary slightly.)

Dolphins of the Sea

The dolphin is a very interesting animal. Dolphins are mammals like us. Did you know that there are 30–40 dolphin species? The bottlenose dolphin is the most common dolphin. Dolphins are like humans, and they are just as interesting.

Page 63 (top)

1. blue (or huge)
2. busy
3. huge (or blue)
4. sweaty
5. soft

Page 63 (bottom)

1–6. Answers will vary.

Page 71

meadow monkeys

in the meadow you will find many animals one of these animals is called the harvest mouse this tiny animal can climb from one plant to another and look just like a Monkey harvest mice climb these Plants looking fore food they eat as much as they can in the summer for winter the harvest Mouse scampers through the meadow along with all the other animals

snake in the grass

snakes are some of the scariest animals the european grass snake is not poisonous, but they can make an awful smell to scare enemies away the grass snake likes to lay in the sun grass snakes eat frogs and newts they live in marshy meadows sometimes the the grass sanke will pretend to be Dead. The more you learn about snakes, the less scary they are

Page 72

1. Dolphins are good swimmers.
2. Are lions, cats, and tigers from the same family?
3. Many bugs buzz and fly around.
4. Do turtles and fish eat them?
5. There are many animals that we can't see.
6. Dolphins are mammals just like us.

Page 101

1. The fly buzzes.
2. The butterfly flutters.
3. The snake slithers.
4. The mountain lion roars.
5. The snail creeps.
6. The leopard stalks.
7. The chick peeps.

Page 103

1. The sky is blue.
2. The ants follow each other in a line.
3. The grasshopper jumped high.
4. The moose was stuck in the river.
5. The peacock is very noisy.
6. The koala bear eats leaves.

Answer Key *(cont.)*

7. Studying animals is fun.

Page 105

1. Where is the zoo?
2. Is the dog brown or black?
3. How does the bird fly?
4. What is the cat eating?
5. Who is making that noise?

Page 107

1. fish
2. bird
3. giraffe
4. kitten
5. dog
6. mouse
7. monkey

Page 109

1. swings
2. runs
3. stands
4. hatch
5. lays
6. eats or gathers
7. gathers or eats
8. live

Page 111

1. sharp, grey, green, or huge
2. gray or huge
3. huge, green or grey

4. huge
5. eight

Page 114

1. quickly
2. carefully
3. slowly
4. quietly
5. loudly
6. happily
7. slowly
8. hurriedly
9. hungrily
10. gently

Page 116

1. We, Diego
2. February, Groundhog
3. Kathey, I
4. I
5. Aunt Sally, Friday

Page 118

1. Do iguanas eat fruit?
2. I like to see the swans fly.
3. Is the crane a bird?
4. The bear began to run.
5. It is a book about wolves, bears, and foxes.
6. I saw a planet, a falling star, and the moon.
7. Is Sea World in California, Florida, or Texas?